A Soul
Sista's Issues

Karla E. Mack

A SOUL SISTA'S ISSUES

Copyright © 2020 by Karla E. Mack

Cover design by Feyisayo Benedict (DIGITALI)

Interior design by August Pride, LLC.

Printed in the United States of America

ISBN: 978-1-950681-67-9

Ordering Information:
Quantity sales. Special discounts are available on quantity purchases by corporations, associations, and others. For details, contact the author at the email address below.

Karla E. Mack

Ksample1913@gmail.com

Portrait gift from my friend, Fikayo Babawale (2016)

Photo by Marvin L. Sample, Sr.

In memory of my mother, Wilma Jean Sample. You may be gone but you are not forgotten.

We as Black Americans are not trying to conquer the world through our protests, we are simply trying to be a part of it.

Karla E. Mack, 2020

Minority does not mean no authority.

Karla E. Mack, 2020

ACKNOWLEDGEMENTS

Glory to God. He is awesome! Without Him, I can do nothing.

I express my indebtedness to my parents, Marvin Sample, Sr., and Wilma Sample (deceased), who made every effort to raise me in the most positive environment possible.

Gratitude to my two brothers, Marvin Jr., and Gary Sr., for helping me through some of my less fortunate life situations.

Special love to my two children, TaShauna (daughter) and Kendall (son). Thank you for your support. I am proud of who you have become. I would not trade either of you for the world.

To my husband, Isiah, aka "Booka"—thank you for your unconditional love and genuinely believing in me.

To my cousin, Shatara, I appreciate your help back in the day when I experienced what I referred to as "babysitter crisis." You were a lifesaver!

Thank you to my cousin, Karen, a listening ear.

To my cousin, Toya, though we stay many miles away, it has meant a lot that you check on me from time to time to ensure all is well. Thank you.

Recognition is extended to the following host of friends: Carrie, Delana, Dorissenia, Ebony, Lynn, Monique, Tanika, Teresa, and Vickie—the best friends in the whole wide world. I thank each of you for keeping it real over all the years. When I was down, you lifted me! I am profoundly grateful for the support and love.

Thank you to those who encouraged me to finish my novel. I have picked it up and put it back down for over two decades. Thank you to those who provided critiques. All input was valued.

Finally, thank you to everyone who has purchased this novel. I have been inspired by many people who may never know. They include Michelle Obama, Alfre Woodard, Oprah Winfrey, Tyler Perry, and Alicia Keys.

Enjoy my first novel and look for more to follow. May each of you be continuously blessed.

Author's Note

When I say, "With God all things are possible," I mean just that. I have had some extremely rough moments throughout my life. Through it all, I have always managed to move forward. I refused to make excuses. Excuses hinder! I never pitied in my sorrows. Instead, I surrounded myself around people who valued me and who lifted me.

There were times when I considered myself to have gone through *stationary moments*. I never allowed those moments to set me back.

I want my daughter, TaShauna, to know, I find you to be like me. You are a conqueror. You have visions out of this world! Any of your visions can become a reality. Stay focused!

To my son, Kendall, you have many talents. There are no limits to the things you can achieve in life. You are intelligent. Your inquiring mind will lead you places beyond imagination. Joining the Air Force National Guard Reserves was one of the first manly decisions you made on your own. Stay focused! I know God will bless and protect you because of your bravery and commitment to serve your country. Keep God in your life. You will succeed beyond measure.

I love you both!

Anyone who may be struggling in any area of your life, just know the saying, "Joy cometh in the morning" is a true saying. Keep in mind, no matter what you are going through, there is someone else in a worse situation. Do not pity yourself. Do not make excuses. Believe in yourself! My sincerest prayer is that each one of you reading this book will find joy, peace, and a lifetime of happiness!

How We Met

I have known Isaac since high school. Boy was he the man! I'm talking sexy as hell, tall, dark, smooth complexioned, *and* muscular. No flaws! He was Bakersville High School's varsity quarterback and All-American track star. To sum it up, Isaac was *all* that and then some.

Guess what?

I ended up marrying him. Yeah, that's right. Lucky me.

Isaac and I met during our junior year. I was *his* water girl on the varsity football team. After observing him for two years, I figured it was time to come up with a plan to position myself closer to him. I would see him strutting through the halls from time to time. I had already claimed, *in Jesus' name*, that he was going to be *my* man one day. So, I signed up to be a Varsity Water Girl. God answered my prayers; I was one of the chosen few.

I, Evette Sampson, made a pledge to myself. I would be the *only* one to keep Isaac's thirst quenched. No other player was getting water from my sports bottle except *my* Prince Charming. As far as I was concerned, the rest of the players could look forward to receiving their water from the remaining three water girls: Chasity Gregory, Lorna Nixon, and Michelle Lee. As long as *my* plan was understood, the days were good. In my mind I thought, "Don't start nothing, it won't be nothing."

During homecoming, Michelle Lee, best friends with Football Queen, Quintella Dickerson, hurriedly wobbled onto the field on one of the time-outs to give *my* dream man some water.

I know she didn't.

I stormed on to the field and knocked her big wobbly butt to the ground right in front of the crowd. It was like some demon had taken over inside; my adrenaline was at its highest peak. Before I knew it, Michelle Lee was lying on the ground looking dumbfounded. I never understood why she was chosen to be a water girl anyway. Gym, I thought would have been a better fit.

After that embarrassing episode, Michelle Lee never attempted to give *my* All-American sweetheart any water again. *I guess sometimes an example must be made of somebody to ensure everybody understands potential consequences.* Even though I did no harm to Quintella, who attended the same church as me, she and Michelle Lee avoided me altogether from that point. They referred to me as "bully."

I would not agree with "bully," but I would agree, when it came to *my* boo, I did not take any bull!

The following Monday, I was summoned to Principal Henry's office during homeroom. Consequently, I was suspended for three days. I lost my water girl privileges. I was denied entry to any school related sporting events. Finally, I was informed I could not attend junior prom. I hadn't planned to attend the prom, so I was cool with that, but I felt not being able to attend any sporting events was a little overkill. All I could think about was not having the opportunity to see *my* Prince Charming during the upcoming track season; how I would miss seeing his long sexy, dark chocolate, muscular legs sprint down the track field.

I returned from suspension. After three failed attempts to open the combination lock on my locker, Isaac had managed to hunt me down in the hallway between classes. He had heard the news about the suspension. He asked if I was okay. I disclosed how ashamed I felt for causing a scene at the game. Isaac conveyed how my "psychotic actions" impressed him. He felt my actions indicated how much I really must have liked him. He found everything to be a little "cute."

Isaac said he had never talked to any of the girls at Bakersville High because they were all too prissy. He admired my assertiveness. We talked the remaining two minutes before the bell rung for class. He asked if he could give me a call sometime. I gave him my number.

Yes Lord!

Later that evening, Isaac called. Within weeks we became best friends. Within a month, we were a loving couple.

I reminisced, if I had to do it all over again, I believe I would. My punishment didn't really affect me. My mission had been accomplished. It reminded me of a popular song by Oleta Adams. The way you get there doesn't matter as long as you get there. Well, I got there!

Who needed to be a water girl anymore? Who needed to go to all the games? Who needed to go to the stupid old junior prom?

I had *my* dream man. That was all that mattered!

Isaac and I married exactly one week after graduation. Since I considered *my* prince the sexiest man alive, sex was not an issue. I shared myself with him twenty-four seven! Put it this way...There was love. There was marriage. Then, there was a baby in a carriage.

On that note, college was out for me. I was cool with that. School wasn't my favorite and I never could decide on what career to pursue anyway.

Isaac decided college was out for him too. Even though he had been awarded a football scholarship, he decided not to pursue a football career. I was cool with that. He only played high school football to please his father. After four years of being in the spotlight, Isaac felt the need for a break from all the hype and fame. He purchased an old

Ford work truck and started his own lawn business. As a black man, he felt it was best to make his own money.

Over the next nine years, we produced three beautiful children. First, Isaac Jr., a spitting image of his father. Two years later, JaRon, who had equal similarities between the two of us. Within another two years, Danielle, my spitting image. My father would say, she was "my shadow." Everywhere I went, Danielle was right beside me.

I had my tubes tied after Danielle. Fooling around with Isaac, we could have easily had children every two years at our rate, which would have put us to around five kids by now. I just couldn't get enough of his chocolate affection according to him. I must agree. All I know is this sista here went to work *every* day with a great big smile on her face.

The Bust

Family, friends, and neighbors have always praised Isaac and I on our relationship. We'd be lucky to get through one day without someone somewhere asking what our secret was on remaining such a "loving" couple. We were considered the "happiest family in the world."

True! We were happy. We were happy for nine long fun-filled years to be exact, until Mr. High School Quarterback and All-American track star decided to have an affair.

Yes, an affair!

Not only that, but an affair with our former classmate, former Football Queen, Quintella Dickerson! *How about that?*

I didn't care for Quintella back in school. She was beyond weird; there was no other way to explain her. I never sensed Isaac to be the cheating type. When he cheated, all I could ask was, *why Quintella?*

He put his marriage on the line for *that* weirdo?

I was lost as all get out! *What's wrong with men these days? Do they have any earthly idea when they have someone who is good?*

I was one hundred percent faithful to my Boo Bear. I mean, I would not have cheated on him if someone were to put a gun to my head and demanded it. *That's some deep shit! Faithful...even with a gun to my head!*

Hell, a sista got down in the kitchen cooking for his stupid ass! As a matter of fact, I got up *every* morning at five o'clock, even on the nights we made love up until two to three o'clock in the morning, basically every night. I prepared his breakfast, had his newspaper handy, and had his black, no cream or sugar added coffee sitting on the table. I made his cheating butt lunch for his "departure into the fields" as he proclaimed. I rested for an hour or two just to get right back up to prepare the youngins for school. It doesn't stop there! Faithful ole me went to work too, came home after six neglected hours of telemarketing, prepared dinner, and cleaned up the damn house! I washed his sweaty, funky underwear. Ugh! For him to be a grown ass man, his underwear was filthier than the kids'! *Is that freakin' love or what?*

Out of all people, Quintella, *Miss Holier Than Thou*! To add, she was *our* pastor, Rev. Leon Dickerson's child; his only child at that. We attended Northside Christians for Life Baptist Church. I never imagined she would have slept with someone period, especially someone else's husband!

Bitch!

My mom always told me, "Don't put anything past anyone."

Well damn, that explained why Isaac was very stringent about getting to church on time. He literally rushed us to Wednesday night Bible class like we were the ambulance crew rushing to a crime scene to save the life of a gunshot victim. Also, the dip shit literally forced the kids to participate in the youth choir. Guess who was the choir director? Quintella! There I was thinking what an honor it was to have such a gentleman stepping up as the head of the house, leading his family to church. I had no doubt Isaac was God sent. *Devil sent if you ask me.*

Without further delay, I'll explain how the knucklehead got busted.

Once upon a time, one night after *doing the do*, Mr. Masculine went to sleep, approximately one minute after reaching his usual quick peak. *I guess for every good thing there is something that lacks a little.* He only lasted three to five minutes, but I guess I'd be lying if I said it wasn't a good three to five minutes. Perhaps he would have lasted longer if there wasn't so much foreplay.

Within thirty minutes of obnoxious snoring, Isaac had the nerves to mumble through those full sexy lips of his... *damn were they sexy,* "Quintella, my wife is going to kill me when she finds out about our affair."

9

I laid there in total shock. I would have whacked him upside his perfectly shaped head, but I figured I'd let him enjoy his *last* night in our luxury king-sized cherry wood sleigh bed, with our white satin sheets and goose down comforter, scented with the Cool Water cologne he wore religiously every day.

The next morning, known as day two, Isaac had the audacity to turn towards me and nibble on my neck with his cracked lips and his morning breath and utter the words, "I love you sweetheart."

I swear it took every bit of my Christian strength to keep from shoving his conniving butt to the floor. I despised him, but I loved him. All I could think about was what should I do—Say something or keep my mouth shut?

Society proclaims talking to oneself is not normal. I must have been the most abnormal sista in the world because I had serious discussions with myself. Then it came…the anger, the rage, and the temporary insanity. Out of nowhere…

"Why? How could you cheat on me? How could you cheat on your family? Here we are going to church all happy like we are the freakin' Cosbys, and all along you are screwing Quintella?" I furiously yelled.

Caught by surprise, Isaac asked, "What are you talking about?"

Why do men always play dumb? Who the hell do they think we are?

"You told me yourself you idiot...you said it in your dream! You had an affair with Quintella! Are you gonna act like you didn't?" I shouted back.

I knew when he rolled back over, the naked truth had been revealed.

"You dog! How could you? You dirty, filthy dog!" I continued.

Isaac pushed himself up into a sitting position and swung his feet out of bed. He got up. With tears and guilt in his eyes, he peeked in at the kids across the hall as though he was making sure they didn't hear me arguing with their loving, too good to be true and faithful father: Mr. Family Man, independent worker, Mr. Charity Giver.

What a fake!

After taking a shower, Isaac slipped into his favorite pair of Levi jeans and threw on a green polo shirt. He finally gained enough courage to look at me eye to eye. *Those beady eyes of his, even though they were watery, they still managed to send a quick chill down my spine. Darn him!*

"Honey, you're right. I am so sorry," he acknowledged and apologized.

Really, I did not expect the ding-dong to admit it. *Shit!* I was hoping he would say it wasn't so. I mean it was only a dream and all...

Suddenly, I went numb. I'm sure my heart stopped pumping for like a minute. I also believe I had a brief period of respiratory arrest. I literally died and came back to life!

Lying naked from last night's moment of passion, I took my first breath after my near-death experience and began to break down again.

"I hate you! I hate you! Why?"

When I glanced up, Isaac Jr., JaRon, and Danielle had awakened and were standing there staring at me in the nude. Isaac shamefully brushed his way past them. He said in his most pathetic voice, "I have to go now."

He left me there all alone to face the children. *What a dick!*

I am not sure if the kids were confused as to why their father left so suddenly, or if their confused looks were because they could not grasp why their mama was lying in the bed completely naked. They stood there like three deer facing the headlights of a Chevy truck on a windy fall night.

In a hoarse voice, I did my best to reassure the kids. I explained, "It's okay babies, go back to bed. Everything is alright. Mama and Daddy love you. We will talk later."

Apparently stunned, they slowly about-faced military style, and eased out without asking questions. Thank God!

The Separation

Three days after the bust, Isaac called apologizing *again* for being unfaithful. While my ears were deaf to his apologies, my mind was open to knowing his whereabouts for the previous nights; however, my tongue for once, was on cease mode. I struggled to ask. I wanted to know, but at the same time I didn't; what if he told me he had been over Quintella's?

Realizing the need for a mental escape, I refocused my thoughts on the affair, which led me right back into shaming him.

"You cheated on your wife! You mean to tell me *that* weirdo is worth losing your family? What were you possibly thinking?"

Neither me nor *our* kids deserved to be chastised for his careless mishaps.

Isaac was not confrontational. He knew me all too well from high school; I had moments of temporary insanity. Yeah, I imagine it was cute back when the focus was not on him. I bet it was not cute anymore since he was the recipient of the insanity. If anything, no matter where his conniving ass was, he was likely living on edge, probably sleeping with one eye open.

I babbled on for at least a good hour. As far as I know, he could have put the phone down; he never uttered a word. Perhaps he was at a loss for words; the cat had his tongue. No telling what was going on in his shallow mind. If anything, I'm sure he realized he had burned the wrong sista.

After *my* intense discussion regarding the affair, we agreed it would be best for Isaac to move out and get an apartment. He found one a few blocks from our six bedroom, four and a half bathroom, three car garage, built from the ground up dream home.

Isaac's father, who I'd say was rich, spoiled him. Lamon Singleton was his name. Lamon inherited money from his father, Isaac's grandfather, Mack Singleton, so our house was basically a gift. I didn't care who begot who, and who gave what to who, all I knew was who wasn't starting over, and that was Evette Singleton, daughter of Willie Mae and Marlon Sampson.

During my teenage years, there was something about a cul-de-sac that spiked my interest. My parents drove past them often. I always envisioned having a family with kids. I could see my kids riding bikes and skateboards up and down the street. Our house was located at the inner end of the cul-de-sac next to the one at the center. The previous house burned down due to a faulty air-conditioning system. Based off the report, the owners relocated. The lot had been vacant two years.

After marrying Isaac, we explored a few neighborhoods. Once I saw the lot for sale, I asked if we could have our house built. I was one who liked what I wanted, when I wanted it, *and* the way I wanted it. Isaac honored my request. I loved our little house off West Jackson Street. If I had to move, he could rest assured the house would be moving with me. This sista girl was not going anywhere!

Isaac may not have loved me as much as I thought, but I knew he at least loved his kids. He had been an excellent father. From the delivery room to the house, he never missed a milestone moment. He was there when each of the kids took their first step. He was there when each of the kids said their first word. He was there when each of the kids started their first day of kindergarten. I'd be lying if I said he was a deadbeat.

A week after the separation, Isaac called to see if he could swing by to speak with the kids. With my approval, he came over, gathered the kids, and supposedly explained his big mistake. I hid out in the bedroom. I wasn't ready to see his face. Isaac was sexy. I was mad. I wanted to keep it that way. Though Isaac never uttered a word to me, he managed to talk to the kids about thirty minutes. Evidently, the dick head felt more entitled to provide the kids an explanation than he did his wife. Left me hanging. *Whatever!*

The kids didn't share what was discussed in their meeting with their father. I didn't bother to ask. They seemed to have an awareness that something major had gone down. I knew Isaac had to regret what he had done, but how could he?

What was it about her? How long did the affair go on? Where? When? How many times?

So many questions left unanswered. I guess it didn't matter how many times. Once was enough!

I wondered if Quintella thought I was ignorant of her scandal with *my* man. Surely, she recalled what I did to her friend, Michelle Lee. Like God, what He did for others, He could do for you.

In her case, it would have been what Evette had done *to* others, she could do *to* you! Michelle Lee went down in the football stadium in front of the crowd. Quintella would go down in the church in front of the congregation. Then again, I couldn't help but think maybe she didn't know what had gone down in our humble home. *Hmm....*

I had a lot of cooling off to do; sitting in front of the fan was not getting the job done. My mom, Willie Mae, would have said, "Chile you need a little church."

Well... Northside Christians for Life Baptist Church was not an option. Perhaps the fan was a better alternative. I presumed that after a while the kids would inquire about church. I had been lucky.

"What reason would I give?" I asked myself. I decided I would refer them to their dad; I'd leave it up to him to explain, after all, he was the serpent. I loved my idea!

I had tried my best to live "acceptable in Thy sight" ever since my downfall in high school. I recalled the harsh punishment. "Vengeance is mine says the Lord" popped into my mind every time I thought to seek revenge. Whether Isaac or Quintella, one of the two needed to experience my hurt. As a matter of fact, forget one of the two, both of their asses needed to feel my hurt.

Raised in church, I recalled bits and pieces of the Bible. Also, I recalled scriptures that Willie Mae recited both day and night. Church folk used to say, "It feels like fire shut up in my bones." I recognized the saying had to do with the "Holy Ghost;" it denoted something miraculous was going on inside the body. In my case, it felt like fire was shut up in my bones, but there was nothing miraculous going on. My fire was more like the devil's fire. Hell, the more I thought about it, I realized I literally had been burned!

Day Before Graduation

Time flew. I thought it only flew when fun was involved. Not! Danielle was due to graduate from kindergarten within twenty-four hours. As usual, I returned home after six neglected hours of telemarketing. Physically drained. I headed straight to the kitchen, slammed my purse and keys on the counter, briskly rubbed my hands under some warm water, and powered on the stove and coffee maker. Eventually, I chugged down a cup of black Maxwell House like it was a shot of tequila. Once my energy level escalated to its momentum, I managed to toss the teriyaki marinated chicken in the oven. Thank God I prepped it earlier that morning. Grabbing my purse and keys, I powerwalked down the hallway to the boy's room to set out their clothes for the graduation. From there, I trudged on over to my room. The sight of my bed teased me. Boy, did I long for a cat nap. Instead, I postured up and kept pushing. Willie Mae would have said, "I had so much to do, and so little time to get it done."

I knew it would take at least an hour to beautify Danielle's hair before nighttime. Where along the genetic pathway she got her hair from was an unsolved mystery. She was my spitting image; well…she was until it came to her hair. My hair had always been fragile, thin, and on the shorter side. Isaac was the most gorgeous man I'd ever met, but his hair wasn't the greatest. He wore a ball cap the majority of the time; I am not sure if that played a role.

Danielle's hair was thick and wavy. It literally hung to her mid back. On a good day, it took at least thirty minutes to untangle it; then another thirty minutes to flat iron, comb, and style it. Every time I combed her hair, she carried on like it was the end of the world; she screamed and hollered. I thought about waiting until early morning, but I didn't want her crying on her special day. Ultimately, I took a deep breath, toughed it up like I always did, and mentally prepared myself for the misery.

Days prior, Ms. Joyce Ann brought over the dress she promised to make for Danielle. Ms. Joyce Ann was our next-door neighbor. Her house was the centered house in the cul-de-sac. People in the neighborhood were not allowed to say "Ms. Joyce," they had to say, "Ms. Joyce Ann," or she'd give an evil eye until her name was corrected. She was worthy to be respected.

Oh my, the dress was beautiful! It looked like it could have taken a month to make. It only took one week according to Ms. Joyce Ann. Danielle was going to wear a white dress trimmed with an eyelet pattern. It had an adorable pink heart sewn on the back of it just above the most beautiful bow ever. The dress was designed to land just above the knees and had a poof to it. So, if Danielle wanted to twirl around like most little girls, it flared out. It must have been worth a hundred dollars or more.

Ms. Joyce Ann also made clothes for other kids on the block. She passed out candies and treats to the kids in the neighborhood. Halloween was every day at her house. She was the most generous and precious person I had ever encountered. Pretty darn stylish for an elderly lady: light skinned with no wrinkles, gray curly hair kept short, the cutest little mole on the left of her upper lip, and oh my God, she wore fashionable red Maybelline lipstick religiously. Pushing eighty years of age, Ms. Joyce Ann truly could have passed for sixty.

Overall, Ms. Joyce Ann was an attractive, single, and independent lady. She never wore a frown on her face. Her husband, rewind…her *ex*-husband, left her for a woman ten years younger. *Men!* Ms. Joyce Ann didn't let it bother her; she kept right on going like the Energizer Bunny. As far as she was concerned, it was his loss. She never re-married. She ran a clothing business from the comforts of her own home. Well, she designed clothes and sold them. I tell you, the lady inspired and encouraged me to endure my little unexpected circumstance. If she did it, I figured so could I. Willie Mae would have said, "Looking at someone else's situation can be beneficial in helping you with your own." That could have been true, but I wasn't a psychologist.

Isaac drove over, picked up Danielle, and took her to the shoe store the same day after Ms. Joyce Ann dropped off the dress. He purchased some dainty white shiny shoes with a matching purse, perfect for a five-year-old. The purse just so happened to have a pink heart on the snap where it fastened. For a man—Isaac did know how to pick out the finer things in life. *Darn him!* I remember the day he slid a three-carat marquise diamond onto my trembling finger. He picked out the ring all by himself. At least that's what he led me to believe. It nearly knocked me off my feet, along with several bystanders: the most exciting moment of my life.

If Isaac hadn't screwed up, he could have been around to at least help prepare the boys. I laid out some blue jeans and tie-dyed t-shirts for them. Based off the past, graduation was normally held during school hours, and the kindergarteners were the only classes expected to dress for the occasion.

The boys were extremely happy for their little sister. Isaac Jr. crafted Danielle a handwritten card. He offered for JaRon to sign it. I thought that was nice. The kids bonded well; they hardly fought. The boys received one good ole fashion whooping a few years ago; the kind that would have put Isaac either in jail or would have warranted a DHS visit. They decided to experiment with sticks one day while outside. Put it this way, Isaac's car was their imaginary canvas. Isaac never disciplined Danielle; he left that up to me. I recall slapping her little hands a couple times for getting into small things. Besides those little mischievous moments, we were blessed with some good kids. I

22

wasn't sure if our separation would ruin things. I could only hope and pray not. *Dumb butt!*

I hardly dressed up. Dresses were not my favorite. I preferred pants and blouses, which I only wore to Wednesday night Bible class and to church on Sundays. We hadn't gone to church for about a month. I played hooky. I felt if I went, somebody would get beat down. Therefore, I was either at home or at work. My job required me to wear khaki pants and the company polo shirt. Basically, my clothes were just collecting dust in the closet on the crochet hangers Ms. Joyce Ann fashioned for me. Whenever I wanted to venture off somewhere, they were coordinated by outfits, so it was just a matter of "grab and go." On that note, I decided to wait to pick out my outfit. Like I mentioned, I was tired, and something had to give! Besides, most of the good moms and wives I knew, saved themselves for last anyhow.

The majority of Isaac's dress clothes were still in his closet. I wasn't sure what he'd wear. He was a neat freak, so no matter what, he'd be his usual "Denzel" self. In school, he claimed to have liked my assertiveness. Hmm, I wondered how he would have felt if I had assertively thrown all his clothes to the curb or donated them to charity. I had only lived with Isaac, but I couldn't imagine most men taking up an entire closet with clothes and shoes. He didn't mention anything to Danielle when he picked her up or dropped her off. I figured I'd just have to wait to see what he would have on when the time came.

Ms. Joyce Ann kept the kids earlier after they got out of school. Every now and then she helped me out when I worked. I disliked having others help. Plus, I didn't trust anyone else with my kids. Ms. Joyce Ann constantly reminded me everyone could stand a little help every now and then. I trusted her. Slowly but surely, I learned it was okay. *What are neighbors for, right?*

"Danielle, Jr., and JaRon come back here please," I called out just as the three darted past me coming from Ms. Joyce Ann's, like I was a ghost dwelling in the living room. All three darted back within seconds; so fast they startled me.

"Danielle, go grab your bag of hair supplies so we can get started on your hair for tomorrow. Jr., you and JaRon find some socks and shoes to wear with the clothes I set out for you. Then, the two of you can go ahead and take your showers and get ready for bed," I ordered.

"Okay," they all said simultaneously.

Sometimes I thought I had triplets; they always responded in unison. While Danielle was off grabbing her bag of supplies and the boys were getting their belongings together, I decided to say a quick prayer. I knew Danielle was about to scream and holler. I was already exhausted and a little cranky. I wanted my princess' graduation day to be special. Therefore, I prayed, "Lord, You know I need patience. I ask that You give me strength. Amen."

Graduation Surprise

"Rise and shine, Danielle! Your big day has finally come," I shouted as I gently shook my little princess.

It took longer than expected to finish her hair. The po chile cried and cried; I cried on the inside. Obviously, it was not meant for me to be a beautician. I could have been a mortician; people couldn't talk back, they couldn't cry…Yeah, that would have been right up my alley. I would have been styling all kinds of hair.

Now, I could have sworn I secured Danielle's pink and white polka dot bonnet onto her head. Evidently, it fell off during the night. After the meticulous work this sista put in, I could have sued whatever company that produced the scarf. *A scarf can be pretty, and appealing to the eye and all, but if it fails to do its job, it needs to be removed from the shelf. I mean, people should know kids are going to toss and turn. Hell, adults do! Make a scarf and provide a "guaranteed to stay on" warranty.*

25

Eventually, Danielle's frowns converted to smiles when she saw her new makeover in the mirror. She pranced and twirled around the house as though she pictured herself in her graduation dress. I had to interrupt her fairy tale moment to enlighten her on how bedtime had lapsed, and how morning was just a few snores away.

Finally, my princess made it to bed around 8:45. Bedtime at the Singleton house was supposed to be 8:00 for *all* three kids. Well, unfortunately, we bombed that curfew! I peeped in her room around 9:00; she was still bright-eyed and bushy tailed. I took a second look around 9:15; she was in her wind down mode. When I checked back around 9:30, she was *out like a light in the night*, as my father would say. Though she expressed how she couldn't wait until the day, I literally had to drag her out of bed. *Po baby.*

I recalled when Isaac Jr. and JaRon graduated from kindergarten. I was excited for them; but with Danielle, I was overly excited. My one and only daughter *and* last child was ready to proceed to the first grade.

Before I know it, Isaac Jr. will be graduating from high school, then JaRon, and then Danielle, I thought as my imagination advanced to future realities.

All I could think was, "What would I do when my three bears are all grown up?"

I managed to suppress my emotions. I was proud of my kids, and myself. We were making it without Isaac in the house, though it had been odd without him. I missed his snoring. Odd, but for some reason I did. I missed how I used to kick him with my foot, and he would stop, and then less than a minute later he'd start up again. I literally got a "kick" out of it. *Jerk!*

Isaac kept his kids and helped financially, but it had been a long stressful journey. I still multitasked around the house, watched the kids off to school, made it home on my off days before the kids returned from school, and bought groceries. The list continued. Even on the days the kids had their fun moments with their father, my workload never ceased. *No break for a faithful ole wife like me!*

Breakfast was served. Everyone had pooped. It was about an hour and a half from graduation time. I wanted to set aside my feelings and focus on my princess. I may have cursed from time to time, but I was a praying sista.

"Lord, please help me to set aside my hurt feelings today. Amen." I pleaded.

Thank God I prayed. Danielle was the first to bring up her dad.

"Mama is Daddy going to be at my graduation today?" she asked.

"Yes baby, your daddy is not going to miss his little princess' graduation."

I felt confident enough to assure her that he would not dare miss this occasion.

"Mama is Daddy going to sit with us?" JaRon asked.

Gulp...now, that was a tough one!

"I am not sure JaRon. If not, he may sit close...*Okay?*" I figured I'd ask for validation.

"Yes ma'am," he replied.

Isaac Jr. remained quiet. I was cool with that.

I parked in our usual parent spot. I didn't see Isaac's car, but I knew in my heart the butt head would show up. He had been a loser husband, not a loser father.

"Okay my three little bears, everybody out. Be careful," I commanded in my motherly voice.

Isaac Jr. helped Danielle out of the SUV. He always amazed me; such a mannerable kid.

"Thank you, brother," Danielle expressed her gratitude.

A proud parent moment.

We entered the auditorium; I noticed several seats on the second row in the center area. The boys were supposed to sit with their classes, but I made an exception to that rule. I have been known to make up my own rules.

"Boys sit here. Save a seat for me while I rush your sister to her classroom," I instructed.

There were approximately fifty-three kiddos in the three kindergarten classes combined. I had two minutes to get my little graduate to her assigned section. Pulling Danielle by her arm, I elbowed my way to the letter "S," placed her in line by her last name, and kissed my shadow on her cheek.

"Mama will see you soon princess. You look so beautiful!" I yelled as though Danielle was the only child in the room.

I didn't mean to elbow my way; it was just that Singletons were never late. At least I didn't knock anyone down along the way. I headed back to *my* pre-chosen spot that I had instructed the boys to reserve, but not without thinking about Isaac. I noticed I still hadn't laid eyes on his ass. *Don't play Boo Boo! Don't do it!*

Nearly forty-five minutes lapsed; the special moment finally had come. I got a feeling it would be the first uplifting moment for me since the affair....my little shadow was about to graduate with straight S's all year long. Danielle loved making "S's" on her grade card. She would always say, "I made a "S" like the "S" in my last name." For some reason that always tickled her pink.

29

Then came my angel, in her little white dress, fitting exceptional as expected.

"Next, we have little Miss Danielle Singleton, proud daughter of Isaac and Evette Singleton."

My heart fluttered at the mention of his name.

Where was he anyway? I pondered.

My princess shyly tiptoed to center stage. Isaac Jr. and JaRon leaned forward in their seats to catch every word and moment. Danielle looked out into the audience, obviously in search for a familiar face. The boys and I waved and waved. Isaac Jr. stood up to wave until I swatted for him to sit back down. I had already asked them not to yell out her name; I didn't know what he'd do next. I thought we had good seats, but I guess not. She never even looked our way.

The audience awed as my baby smiled. Danielle's two bottom teeth were in the loving arms of the Tooth Fairy. Their absence made her smile even more adorable. Up until then, no other child had received the awe of the audience, just my princess. Danielle glared with amazement as she looked somewhere else besides our direction. I turned around to see who was receiving all the glory; being that she wasn't looking up to the Heavens. Boom! There *they* were! The jerk had the nerves to come to *our* daughter's graduation with that heffa, —not only that, but I also thought I saw something! ***Hmm...I know I did not see what I thought I saw!***

30

"Lord, I asked You to set my hurt feelings aside today. I didn't ask You for further hurt today," I conversed with the Lord.

I felt the need to remind Him about my prayer.

Fiercely, I turned back around, only to notice Danielle exiting the stage. I didn't *even* get the chance to snap a photo of my little angel receiving her certificate. *How could he? How could he bring her? How could she come?*

Like I hadn't had enough, I reluctantly looked back again. They were leaving the auditorium, holding hands I might add!

"I must be the one dreaming this time," I thought.

I noticed what I thought I had seen the first time was true. Ms. Thang wa*s* EXPECTING! I blinked a couple of times. She walked like she could have been in labor. *Surely not so! The nerve of him!* ***Bastard! Bastard! Bastard!***

I could no longer focus on the ceremony. It was like my daughter's graduation was no longer a priority. It was, but at the same time it wasn't. The dick did not even stay around to hug his kids! I really thought he'd at least have a bouquet of flowers for his one and only daughter! He probably left early because he knew I would have literally slapped him, and probably would have slapped hoochie mama as well. *Ugh*!

31

My afternoon had just been ruined. I still had a full day ahead. I promised Danielle we would go to Ms. Jean's Pizza and Hamburger Station; the only place in town that sold both pizza and hamburgers. The pizza was the bomb, as the kids would say, which basically meant it was out of this world. I also promised a movie. It had been months since we had seen one as a family. *Player* and I were together then.

I didn't know whether to run after them, run away out the side emergency exit, scream out loud, or sink down in my extra hard folding seat. Ghetto ass stuff like that makes it hard for someone who tries to live a Christian life. For some reason, I wanted to go after Quintella more than Isaac.

What was going on? What did I do wrong?

I guess that's why they say in church to stay prayed up.

She was brave *and* bold coming to *our* daughter's graduation, pregnant at that! Isaac was brave *and* bold for bringing her! We were only separated by the way. We were not divorced! *How trifling!*

Once again, there I was stuck with the three kids, while Daddy was adding sin after sin to our "for better or for worse" commitment. I felt like the Lord failed me. Willie Mae would have scolded me if she had heard me fault the Lord. I mean, what was the purpose of praying if it didn't work?

Was I being punished for something I did over nine years ago? Was that considered one of His mysterious ways?

I needed answers! I didn't know how much more I could take!

Another Day

Thump. Thump.

I felt my pulse. I touched my nose, ear, and chin, just like Willie Mae had me do in front of friends and family back in the day, to boast to the world that her two-year-old daughter was a genius. I was alive! Hallelujah!

"I survived yesterday's torture!" I shouted.

Nothing like a mama pulling through for her kids. Even though I didn't photo shoot Danielle during her once in a lifetime kindergarten graduation, I had an opportunity to take several pictures of her in front of the school after it was all said and done. Though I had purposely avoided church, I knew the Sunday following graduation was when the special program for all graduates was held.

Speaking of church, I couldn't wait! Who cared I hadn't been in over a month? You'd think someone would have called to see if I were okay. Was I on the sick and shut in list, or the AWOL from church list? Maybe I wasn't considered special. It always irked me when someone went missing, everyone be like, "Where is such and such?" Someone else goes missing and no one seems to give a damn. Another thing, a bridal shower would be thrown for one member, and then, another member could get married five times and never have the luxury of a shower.

Church folk!

I had planned to be there alright; whether they had called me or not. Other than at baptisms, graduates were rewarded with a Bible with their names engraved on them. I knew my princess was going to get hers! *Hell yeah!*

I was more motivated to go to church for unrighteous reasons rather than righteous. I was gonna get my chile's Bible, then Sista girl was gonna stand up in front of the entire congregation at Northside Christians for Life Baptist Church and let Rev. Dickerson know all about his little Pumpkin. He referred to Quintella as his little Pumpkin. *More like his little tramp if I had to name her!*

I came to the realization, not all church folk are godly people. Church folk are sinners…. Well, some are. I'm sure Rev. Dickerson wasn't too proud of his little Pumpkin anymore, **pregnant…and not married?** Hmm…. I wondered if that was why he said Quintella would be away for a while. He claimed she would be absent momentarily to pay a visit to her mom for a few months.

Did he know she had made it back?

It was obvious she was pregnant, couldn't hide it. *Was his story a cover up?* Hmm… I may have been the only fool!

I bet Queen B. hadn't stood up in front of the congregation and confessed her sins. Her ass was probably right up there directing the choir like she had set the best example for the youth. The Singleton children were out! They attended church on overnight slumber weekends, but there was no way in hell I was going to allow my babies to be back under her so-called leadership.

I needed to shake my shitty thoughts. I found myself being more of a hateful person. One moment I was mad about the graduation, then I was happy to be alive, and then, I was right back to plotting how I was going to get vengeance while in the Lord's house. I was so outdone; it was getting out of hand. What else could I have done? I had lost ten pounds, my skin was breaking out, and my hair had reached what I referred to as "a Rogaine emergency state."

I said I would never wear a wig; for the first time I was contemplating the possibility. Pebble's Weave and Wig Beauty Store was only a block from the house. Every day I was tempted to stop by. I got braids once. I said I'd never get those rascals again ever since my best friend, Deshaun, put some in so tight, they made my eyeballs pop out. I figured a fool had to be mighty desperate to wanna have lengthy hair, just to have to take narcotic pills for freakin' pain relief. Bless her heart, I mean it took nine hours for her to install my braids; I must have had them in one day, and then the shit had to come out! It took five hours to take the darn things down! Deshaun and I remained best friends, but she said she'd never do anything to my hair again. Believe me, I was cool with that.

I had never tried a weave; I heard they caused people's heads to itch to death. Nothing like a cranky sista, with short nails, with an itchy head, on a hot summer day. Sistas I've seen, go around looking all good, while at the same time they are uncomfortable as all get out. Shit, who has time for that? The things sistas go through. *Life!* I figured if I ever gained the nerves to stop by Pebble's, I would investigate to see if there were any additional options.

The kids were with Isaac for the day. He picked them up every few days. He'd text, "coming for kids" each time. I'd reply with a time for him to have them back. It was bold of him to ask one day after knowing he had pissed me off again; especially knowing I could go temporarily insane at the drop of a dime. Maybe he thought I could go psycho and hurt the kids, so to him, it was worth asking to free the kids…. who knows? I had crazy moments, but I had limits. I could control my crazy like a man could control the TV remote during the Super Bowl. Nothing would make me hurt my kids. I'd own up to crazy. He could own up to stupid!

The New Arrival

While tending to routine household chores, I heard that familiar knock on my front door. I have never been able to figure out why Sophia Potts had to pound so hard. Her knock sounded like she was attempting to escape from a serial killer who had just entered through her back door. Sophia was my neighbor directly across from our house. My nosey neighbor. Every neighborhood had at least one.

Sophia had to weigh at least a good whopping three hundred pounds and then some. She maintained a short burnt-orange afro that resembled the texture of the wig worn by Bozo the clown. *For real!* She was hardly seen without her big, hooped earrings that seemed to coordinate with every piece of attire worn. She was dark complexioned and wore red rimmed glasses that clashed with her afro. She loved the heck out of some bright red lipstick. Perhaps the lipstick complimented the eyeglasses. Who knows?

Majority of the time she wore what my mother called "gaucho pants" back in the day, with loud colored shirts such as lime, yellow and orange. She enjoyed sporting a selection of flip flops that revealed her crusty heels. I mean her heels hung off the back of her shoes about a half inch! Why folk wear shoes that reveal their heels beats the hell out of me. I was *not* cool with that.

Sophia spent at least seventy five percent of her days sitting on her front porch, obviously gossiping on her cordless phone that evidently had an everlasting battery life. She never married, had no kids, but was one who knew everything, especially how to run a marriage and a family. She loved to keep things stirred up in the hood. Of all people, I knew Sophia had to know the scoop on Isaac and me, as far as the affair.

I took long strides to the door to spare damage to my eardrums. In her left hand she held the daily newspaper. Sophia lost her right hand in a devastating car accident several years ago, along with her oldest brother, Carl. A semi-truck lost control and ran into them from the side, pinning Sophia's car up against a cement wall on the highway. By the time the rescue squad arrived at the scene, Carl had died from a massive head injury. Sophia on the other hand, was blessed to walk away with at least one hand. Fortunately, she was left-handed. The rest of her injuries were deemed minor. I heard through the grapevine she hadn't been the same since. That could be why she was the way she was. I didn't know.

"I saw Quintella had a baby girl" were the first words of greeting that parted from Sophia's bright red lips, said in such a way to stir up trouble. I never told her our business; somehow, she found out. I instantaneously snatched the paper out of her hand. Of course, she had it on the birth section. It was true…. a baby girl, born May 8th, exactly one month after Danielle's birth date…. six pounds, eleven ounces. Her name was Shantel Alexandria Dickerson. For some reason, the word *SAD* flashed across my mind; sad but true. Isaac and Quintella were listed as parents. I did my best not to call the baby's mama out of her name. Someone out there had been praying for me!

The paper company had gone an extra step and added "proud parents." The baby at least had Quintella's last name. *Shew!* At that point, I didn't think I could stand it being Singleton. Thoughts crossed my mind.

How does the baby look? Is she really Isaac's baby? Maybe Quintella could have laid with someone else's husband too.

Then thoughts of the actual delivery process invaded.

Were they holding hands as Quintella pushed? What was Isaac saying to her for support? What was his fatherly reaction when the baby came out?

Suddenly a sense of nausea approached. I figured it was time to shorten Sophia's visit. I said, "Thanks for the paper."

I really think her intentions were just to show me; she dared to take it back at that point. "I guess I better finish cleaning before the kids come home," I made an excuse to sum up the visit.

Sophia turned around, wobbled towards the door, but being the instigator she was known for, she had to say one last thing before she made her get away…. "Looks like Isaac had himself a little cake *and* a little icing too."

Then she made her annoying giggle sound. It took tremendous effort to ignore the comment as I said once more in my high pitch, nice, but you are about to piss me off voice, "Thanks for stopping by! See you later!"

"Tootles". ….my old classmate Vickie would say.

Sophia had good intentions for the most part. Everyone in the neighborhood really enjoyed having her around. She was our neighborhood watch person. We couldn't live with her, but really didn't desire to live without her. I must admit a few burglars landed their criminal, not wanting to earn their own shit, asses in jail because of Ms. Sophia's nosey spying self.

I returned to my chores. The kids had arrived from their weekend church event. Every third Friday and Saturday of each month always seemed to be the fastest twenty-four hours. Gee, I hardly got a break. Sometimes little princess would go, other times she wept to stay home with her mama; however, she went that time. She must have felt the need to have a break from me, *huh?* I think it was because she wanted to wear her new outfit. Her grandma, Betty Singleton, had sent her a jumper and some matching sandals for her graduation gift. I had never heard of people giving clothes for graduating from kindergarten, but hey, at least she thought of her granddaughter.

"Hi Mom!"

"Hey Mom!"

"Hello Mama!"

All three yelled as they leaped into my arms like puppies greeting their owner who had just arrived home after a hard day's work.

"Mom, we saw Daddy and the baby," Isaac Jr. informed.

He was the spokesperson for the bunch. He kept me updated on everything that took place during each sleep over. He was sort of like a miniature Sophia—full of information, sometimes providing more than a person desired to know. I had to listen though. He was just too full of excitement to cut off.

"So, your dad was back at church?" I asked.

He hadn't been back there since he was busted.

"No, he came to pick up Ms. Quintella and we saw him," Jr. corrected my assumption.

Isaac Jr. took his little polaroid camera everywhere he went, just like his grandpa, Marlon. He went on to say he had the opportunity to take pictures of his half-sister, Shantel.

I knew the baby was innocent and all, but I'll admit, I resented her just a tad… just a tiny, tiny bit.

JaRon, not knowing any better, blurted out, "Mom, she looks just like you!"

Yikes! On that note, before the unpredictable sequence of shocking news continued, I asked Danielle if she had something to add. She didn't. As my shadow, she must have felt my pain. Usually smaller children get more excited. Danielle did not…she wa*s my girl.*

All I thought to say was, "Well, hopefully you'll each grow to love your new little baby sister. I am sure she is adorable."

Pugh!

I told the kids to go put up their belongings and to get their clothes ready for church. I still had not stood up in front of everyone to put in my two cents. I had a feeling that Sunday may just be the Sunday. I chickened out the last time. I left after Danielle received her Bible. Quintella wasn't there anyway. Supposedly, she had the baby. This time, however, I figured I'd put on all my jewelry just in case I got into a fist fight. That's how a sista felt. I just wanted to beat a sista down. Christian life wasn't easy by any means. I tried and tried, but like the song implied, I need others to be patient with me. God was not done working with me yet. Until I came forth as pure gold, I knew I'd be wearing *all* my gold, just in case I needed to add a few permanent marks to Quintella's face! Even the holiest earthly creature

44

has a little ghetto within. Surely Jesus thought of a few things He could have done when He walked the face of the earth, but being perfect, He just did not act upon them. Well, to set the record straight…Evette Singleton was NOT JESUS!

Summer Break

School was out for the summer. It hadn't registered I'd have the kids all day every day unless I hired a sitter; that was a big N to the O to the P to the E; not in my budget! Ms. Joyce Ann only kept the kids a few hours here and there. So wrapped up in the recent drama, I was oblivious to the future. While uncertain if I could talk rationally with Isaac, at least for five minutes, it was mandatory I called. We needed to establish a plan for the kids. He made good money in the lawn business; surely, he could afford something. Hell, I needed help. One thing for sure, Baby Shantel wasn't going to be robbing from *my* kids; *my* three were here first!

Two days had gone by; reluctant, but I finally struck up enough nerve to call Isaac. Apparently, his ass wasn't going to call me. *Men are good at that shit...avoiding the first call, like women are at fault in their situation.*

My fingers trembled, my palms suddenly became sweaty as I managed to tap out the digits to his cell phone, hoping his egg head wouldn't think I was calling to beg for him to come home. *Not!*

Isaac answered after one ring. "Hello."

I heard his deep baritone voice. *Whew!* Without hesitation, I informed him we needed to discuss summer plans for the kids.

As though I hadn't said a darn word, he asked, "How are you?" and stated, "I miss you Evette."

"I'm fine," I replied bluntly, avoiding the second part.

I simply repeated my initial concern, staying focused on my mission. I wanted to say, *miss you too, get your butt home*, but I wasn't going out like that. I reminded him of my work schedule, and that Isaac Jr. wasn't quite old enough to baby-sit, as if he didn't already know. I suggested camp.

Isaac responded, "Evette you know I'll do whatever it takes to help you out. Just let me know what you need, and I'll be there for you."

So basically, between all the mack lines, the bucket head pleasantly left everything up to me. *Men!*

"Okay, I'll see what *I* can arrange," I said with emphasis on the word I. "I'll call you back once I find out something," I added.

Isaac, with his ongoing flirtatious remarks, said, "Okay sweetheart, love you and have a good evening."

Now, what the hell was he up to? He must have thought he was Denzel Washington!

Upon hanging up the phone, chills shot down my spine. Out of the blue, tears began to stream down my cheeks as I realized how much I really missed his ole funky butt. I guess I really hadn't cried much. In fact, I hadn't cried at all. So, for the next three and a half hours, I cried my little heart out. My cup runneth over.

Crying alleviated a little bit of the pressure in my chest. "Isaac is going to mess around and cause me to have a heart attack if I am not careful," I pouted and whined to myself.

I never cried so hard in my nine years of marriage. Tears would be of joy, not freakin' sorrow. Indeed, a first! After thinking about it further, I could not recall the last time I cried. Maybe it was when Danielle was born? I really could not remember!

The church was having youth summer camp. I just didn't feel *my* kids needed any more of the Northside Christians for Life Baptist Church than they were already receiving. I didn't want them to become too holy. Too holy folk were beginning to scare me. I was sure somebody out there would understand.

After reading through the school bulletin sent home in JaRon's backpack, I decided I'd check into Camp Versatile. The camp offered cheerleading, martial arts, and photography classes, in addition to many others. After checking into it, the price was reasonable, and the hours accommodated my needs. The camp offered classes the kids would enjoy. Danielle loved cheerleading, JaRon loved karate chopping his way around the house, and Isaac Jr. had an overwhelming interest in photography. Perfect!

The next day, I placed another call to Isaac to inform him what *I'd* recommend. Of course, he was okay with *my* recommendation. He claimed to have heard good news about the camp already from an old buddy of his. He thought it was an affordable choice. This time before the conversation came to a yield, Isaac complimented me on my parenting.

"You're a wonderful mother, Evette. The kids could have no better mom than you."

"Thank you. I guess you are an okay father," I sarcastically responded.

I said "Bye" and hung up before he could mumble another word.

"Duh! Not only a wonderful mother, jack ass; but also, the best damn woman you'll ever find. Tell me something I don't know. Screwball!" I hollered, immediately realizing I slammed the phone down on the wrong end.

I could tell Isaac was missing me. They say people don't realize what they have until it is gone. Why some folk must learn the hard way beats the hell out of me. I refused to let him know I missed him. My classmate, Vickie, taught me—sometimes women must act like they don't give a rat's ass before these knucklehead men come to their senses. I never understood what a rat's ass had to do with anything, but it sounded fitting.

Five weeks later….

The kids were down to one more week of Camp Versatile. Then, they had one free week before they were due back to school. Summer had gone by faster than lightening could strike during a spring storm; it seemed like I blinked and then it was time to prepare for the return of school. My little calendar organizer was no longer organized. Every day was double booked with a task of some sort. Talking about stress at its best!

The last Friday was time for the kids to show what they learned in camp. The theme was "Show Yo Folk What You've Been Working With." To be a predominately white camp, they had a little ghetto touch to their theme. Isaac anticipated coming, according to Danielle, which didn't surprise me. My nerves started going one hundred miles per hour. I hadn't physically seen Isaac since the graduation. Would he bring Queen B.? *Surely not!*

I found myself having uncontrollable panic attacks. During all my busy, running around, I took a trip to see my physician *and* counselor, Dr. Gregg. You could say, I was blessed with two specialists in one. She prescribed me some Xanax. It was an anti-anxiety medication.

She felt it would minimize my temporarily insane moments. I was not fond on taking prescription medications, too many famous folks seemed to have trouble with addictions. Maybe it was just narcotics; but who knows? I was sure that poor old non-celebrity gals like me could get addicted as well. However, a sista had to do what a sista had to do to maintain; I had to keep those nerves of mine in check. Lord knows I did not want to go off the deep end. *Life must go on, right?* Dr. Gregg emphasized I would not have any trouble as long as I took the Xanax as prescribed. For once, I had to follow rules.

I didn't have too much sista pride to acknowledge the need for a little mental assistance. After nine years of faithfulness on my end…The shit was real! My few friends during my school days used to say, "Girl you are so crazy," back when I plotted to win over *my dream man.*

I guess I put the "legit" in legitimate—crazy me.

Willie Mae assured me, "To solve a problem, one must confess to having one."

Well, I had my share. Willie Mae would add, "If you never had a problem, you wouldn't know that God could solve them."

I had no doubt God was okay with me taking Xanax for the time being, until He could come up with His solution for me. Thinking of it that way made me feel better about myself. I had faith God would have mercy on poor little sinful ole me, and He would carry me through the wilderness…That was if I refrained from beating down

Quintella. He was known to come on time, all I could say was His time needed to be sooner than later. If not, I could see myself counting on Xanax for life. I'd have to get used to the wilderness.

A Date with the Mate

Why on Earth did I accept a lunch date with Isaac? It was like setting myself up for mass destruction.

Well, here's what happened…

Upon leaving the camp performance, Isaac offered to take me to my favorite restaurant. His invitation was hard to decline. He claimed he was ready to enlighten me on all the nitty gritty. In other words, he was ready to spill his guts about the affair.

Finally!

I may have been somewhat depressed; but my appetite was not affected one bit. I hadn't missed any meals. I figured I'd pop a Xanax and go with the flow.

Marie's Dine-in Soul Food Family Restaurant was off the chain. Though located deep within the ghetto, the food made you disregard the bullets flying outside the window. Customers willingly risked their lives to eat there. We did too. Isaac and I would just strap on our bullet proof vests and take our chances. I'm kidding, but we did have to pay attention to our surroundings.

I was determined to fix up for the date. I wanted his cheating derriere to believe I had been taking excellent care of myself. The last couple of times I hadn't looked as sexy as I preferred, even though it was not like Queen B. was any competition. I mean, hoochie mama had long natural hair and all, but a long ass Pinocchio nose to accompany it. The weirdo was slim, you know, one of those who could slip in a crack on a sidewalk if she didn't pay attention to where she was going. And she wore oversized clothes; you'd think she had on Sophia's hand me downs. Perhaps it was a preacher's daughter's thang and I wouldn't understand, part of the holy family look.

Gee, I was extremely curious to know how the affair surfaced!

I concluded that the rendezvous would either bring us closer together or push us further apart.

"Hmm, should I wear something I already have? Or should I go purchase something Isaac has never seen me wear?" I debated.

I favored the second thought. I wanted him to know that a sista was handling her business. I even decided I'd tighten up a few things if you know what I mean. Isaac was my Denzel; maybe I could be his Beyoncé for once.

56

I browsed around for three hours, only to circle back to the first store in which I started. The kids hated shopping with me, especially when it came to back to school shopping. Unlike their father who would just be in and out, I'd literally go back to the same stores over and over. As a result, I went shopping alone the majority of the time. I was cool with that.

My selection was on point. I chose a black scooped-neck-silk blouse with a low cut back, and a matching pair of black leather pants. I ran across some nice half inch black pump shoes. They had gold specks across the top which complimented my gold jewelry. I usually only wore make-up on formal or semi-formal occasions, but I planned to throw on a dab of make-up too for my boo. I headed to the Maybelline section and put my trust in the cosmetician to hook me up. I decided I'd change up my perfume to make him wonder where it came from. Nothing like giving him a little something extra to think about. *I was loving this ordeal.*

After maxing out my MasterCard, I headed home, laid out my outfit, set aside my makeup, and prayed for a good night's sleep. I felt like a child, antsy about going on a long-awaited trip to Disney World. I needed beauty rest, so I would not only look like the diva I imagined, but also so that I would feel my best. I knew Mr. Man would be sharper than a double-edged sword. *Damn!* He would be hot as hell no matter what. His knucklehead butt would look sexy in a mixed match sweat suit with a hole in one knee and grass stains embedded in the other. The only thing that would make a head turn away from him would be some obnoxious body odor. But…that could be fixed if that were a problem.

I recalled Danielle on the night prior to graduation. She had trouble winding down due to excitement. Same here, it took me forever to wind down, even after taking a Xanax. I felt like I was going on my first date again. Something about Isaac always made me tremble. I almost cared less about the affair. It was going to be just us two, *my* time now, potential for a new beginning.

Was this love or stupidity? *For better or worse, huh?* I longed to see what direction this date would take us.

The day had come. Morning had gone by. Kids were at their designated destinations. *Man, I was so glad Ms. Joyce Ann taught me to accept help!*

I was kicked back, waiting on Denzel's twin to come to my rescue. I took a half dose of Xanax. My nerves had been swimming around like Nemo looking for his father. I figured a half one wouldn't interfere with my mental thinking.

Knock. Knock.

There he was, on time as usual. I slowly made my way to the door. I didn't want to look too eager. I checked my make-up, peeped at my hair in the back…nothing like pieces going the wrong direction. Finally, I took a quick peek in my nose and made sure there were no green action figures dangling around. I remembered my so-called friends in school. They would refuse to inform me when I had something in my nose. I had to discover it later. Then, I spent hours tracking my every move to figure out how long it could have possibly been there. I hated that!

I opened the door and put on my exaggerated grin.

"Hello beautiful queen. Girl, you look stunning!" Isaac complimented before I could verbally greet him.

He looked mighty handsome himself. He presented me with twenty-four lovely red roses in an exquisite looking vase.

"Thanks," was my quick response.

I kept it simple and short, even though I wanted to pull him up to me and start off kissing his juicy lips, perhaps leading to other romance.

"Are you ready?" Isaac asked.

"I imagine so," I replied.

Off to the little black BMW we went. Why did I suddenly visualize Quintella sitting in the passenger's seat? Ooh, if I were a man at that moment, my hard on would have been ruined right then and there. If he weren't treating me to my favorite restaurant, I would have copped out. I'd come too far to turn back.

As we pulled away from the curb, Isaac mentioned again how stunning I looked. He said I looked like I was maintaining well. *Little did he know.* He must have sensed I was wearing a different perfume; he complimented the scent. I ended up borrowing a little of Ms. Joyce's…I mean Ms. Joyce Ann's perfume. She had brought it back from a trip she took to Germany many years ago. She called it "Germany's Special" because there was no name on the bottle, and she had forgotten the actual name of it. Ms. Joyce Ann had my back. She knew how men were firsthand. Remember, her husband left her for a younger woman.

Anyway, I finally put aside my selfishness; I complimented Isaac's handsomeness and emphasized how it was a pleasure to see him. I thanked him again for the roses. He knew I loved roses. He would buy me roses just because. I didn't have to wait for special holidays. My Boo Bear had been a charmer since day one.

The closer we got to the restaurant the more my stomach rumbled from starvation. I couldn't wait to eat my mouth-watering fried pork chops, mustard and collard greens mixed, and Marie's to die for red beans and rice. Soon to follow, I knew I would be eating her outstanding peach cobbler! I didn't care much for peach cobbler, but Marie's was one I'd eat every day if I had the recipe. Oh, wait a minute; I can't forget to include the hot water cornbread. You ain't had no hot water cornbread until you had Marie's. Talking about being on cloud nine, I could not tell if it was the Xanax or the fact the food was working on my taste buds.

Isaac and I always ordered the exact same meal. Everyone at the restaurant knew us. We didn't have to place our order; they ordered for us. All I knew at that point was that Queen B. better not had been to *our* favorite eating spot! It was enough knowing her anorexic butt had been in my passenger's seat.

Lord knows she better not have been to our restaurant! Isaac will be as dead as the meat is on the menu's special. It is that serious! She done had enough of my goodies already. I conversed with myself as usual.

Players back in the day took two different women to the same place. *What was up with that?* When busted they couldn't even begin to explain their way out. *Come on...at least go to two different places for goodness sake!* One psycho took a friend of mine and another woman to the same movie on different dates, and his ass sat there and acted like he had never seen the movie. Funny. Crazy! But I knew my prince charming wasn't like that. I really did. Not *my* Isaac pooh. Surely, he was better than that.

Up Close and Personal

Back towards our little once happy home on West Jackson Street, Isaac and I mutually agreed that home was the best place to initiate his long-awaited confession. We decided we didn't want anyone at the restaurant to detect we were having marital problems. Plus, we wanted to enjoy our meal. I was cool with that. All I needed to do was padlock my vagina to keep from sexually attacking him. A sista's hormones were raging… but, then they suddenly halted.

Realization hit! Isaac didn't use protection with ole girl. Yuck! I got over that temptation; nothing like my own husband passing a STD to me, charming folk can catch STDs. ***Bastard!***

One minute I was in love; the next minute I felt like committing murder. Then, one minute my heart raced from excitement; the next minute it raced due to anger. Let the truth be known, there was a thin line between love and hate.

How long would I have off and on emotions? Would they ever end?

I was determined to ride out the occasion. Lord knows, I needed to hear what could have possibly led my husband to sell out.

As Isaac pulled into the driveway, I reached over to the sun visor on his side of the car. I pressed the button to the garage door opener so Isaac could drive straight in. Sophia was likely to see us; I didn't want to deal with her nosiness. She took the meaning out of comforts in your own home. Sometimes I found myself tiptoeing around like she could hear my footsteps from across the street. It wouldn't have surprised me. *Sad, isn't it?*

We proceeded to the bedroom for discussion. Isaac claimed there were no strings attached. He just wanted to chat in the bedroom. I mentioned before, he was smooth in his ways. Regardless, just thinking about Queen B., my vagina was in relax mode.

Isaac thanked me for such a wonderful time. He expressed that no matter what, I was the love of his life. He pre-apologized for what he was about to confess. My Xanax was still in effect.

He began by saying Rev. Dickerson had always wanted Quintella to be with him. He said from the very beginning of our marriage, Rev. Dickerson had pushed his daughter on him.

What the hell? Well, I'll be damned!

After we were married for some time, the pressure died out. However, within the last year or so, Quintella had been feeling as though she'd be single the rest of her life. Supposedly, little Miss Pumpkin had been in bad relationship after bad relationship and had not found Mr. Right.

Rev. Dickerson had the nerves to pull Isaac aside one Wednesday night after Bible class when I wasn't there. He asked Isaac if he would assist in encouraging his someone else's husband seeking daughter in believing there was a good man out there for her.

Did she ever pay attention to her father's sermons? Hell, he often preached about waiting on God to mold your soul mate for you. Let alone, did he practice what the hell he preached?

Anyhow, Isaac admitted he agreed to talk to Quintella, being a gullible gentleman. So, that night after Bible class, he drove her home; that's where the story began. Quintella resided in a studio house just behind her father's house. Rev. Dickerson was divorced. Reportedly, he was divorced prior to his calling to God. I didn't have the details on his marriage, obviously it was not too good; he was single!

Quintella poured her weak heart out to *my* baby about being lonely and feeling unworthy. *My* boo in returned tried to lift her spirits by telling her how wonderful she was…

Blah, Blah, Blah…

Eventually, she started crying, being a big wuss, putting on an overly distraught act. Isaac being all sympathetic, grabbed her and held her. From there, one thing led to another.

At that point, I cut Isaac off and asked, "How many times?"

His response was, "Once and once only baby…she knows you are my one and only."

He made it clear he only brought her to the graduation to prove he'd be there for her and be supportive of his child. He pointed out, Quintella convinced him just before his unprotected climax, she couldn't get pregnant. Following the one-night stand, Isaac immediately expressed to Quintella that what had just happened between them was a mistake.

It was a mistake alright!

After that, I believed *my* boo. I didn't care to know anything else. He was still in hot water with me though, but I had enough of that fairy tale! It was more like a nightmare without it being on Elm Street.

I thought I attended the best church in the world. I assumed all along Rev. Dickerson would be ashamed that his little Pumpkin got pregnant. Not only that, but she got pregnant by a married man *and* prior to wedlock. If that ain't three sins in one, then my name ain't Evette Singleton.

All alone, his hypocrite Jesus wanting to be ass, had played a part in the affair as far as I was concerned. It was really time to stand up in front of the church. I had put it off long enough! Testimony time was a few days ahead for real! Isaac was given the first invite. His attendance was expected! So, come to find out, I was the only one surprised by all of this!

Ever been there?

I was the darn fool! *What did I do to deserve this?*

I never understood why good folk had to go through so much turmoil. Bad folk seemed to have it easier, even though they'd have to answer to the Lord. I wondered what the Lord would say to Rev. Dickerson. I wasn't going to sit around and wait to find out, I knew what I was gonna say!

Follow me to North Side Christians for Life Baptist Church. A church where the motto was "Everybody is Somebody."

Hmm...somebody alright. Somebody crooked!

Testimony Time at North Side

Devotion began about fifteen minutes late, our church norm. It was not unusual for the deacons to spend up to thirty minutes singing songs, praying, reading scriptures, and singing again. Church could have really been over after devotion, but after devotion was announcements. There went another fifteen to twenty minutes. Luckily, the kids had youth church because Danielle would surely have been sleep by the time the announcements were over.

After announcements, there was prayer. *Didn't Deacon John just pray?*

Everyone who had issues had to stroll down and tell their life story, or at least tell their neighbors, their co-workers, their friends, or friend's friend, and so on. No telling how many more minutes that added. I was so ready for Rev. Dickerson to come out, I just wanted to say, "Let's be done already!"

Isaac met me for church. He knew I had threatened to stand up. I have been known to be unpredictable. He didn't know whether to believe me or call my bluff. I am sure he was about to pee his pants. As he stood next to me, I began contemplating how I wanted to go about the bust:

Before the sermon, during the sermon, or during the invitation? All I knew was I was ready to speak my mind, right up in the Lord's house.

Finally, the choir sang their two selections. The preachers strutted in from the side door next to the choir stand. They wore their Sunday's best: two-piece suits with coordinated shoes, ties, and handkerchiefs. Personally, I thought only the choir marched in. That had been an added modification since my last attendance. Something new. I guess the preachers wanted to make a special parade style entrance.

"Wait! What the heck," I muttered.

Rev. Dickerson was NOT in the line!

As church proceeded, the congregation was informed Rev. Dickerson had another engagement at another church in another part of the city. *Dang it! Ugh!* And, to add, Quintella was not there either! *God must have been all up in the middle of that! That was the second time it had happened.*

70

I was ready to go before Assistant Pastor Samuels could announce his subject for the day. His subject was titled, "The Devil is a Liar." I was pissed! Pissed, right in church, aisle five, left section, second seat from the right, just behind Sr. Geraldine Buckingham, who angelically modeled her pink wide-brimmed feather net church hat, and some white laced gloves up to her elbows. *This could not be happening!*

I looked at Isaac; I could tell he knew exactly what I was thinking. He thought it would be a perfect time to place his arms around my neck and rub my shoulder. I quivered from frustration.

Leave or not leave? That was my question.

I decided to stay since the kids were already settled in their classes. Plus, I wanted to look around at other church folk to see if I could vibe that anyone else knew what had gone on. *Was I really the only fool in the church?*

Pastor Samuels started off with the usual, "God is good all the time."

The church congregation responded, "and all the time God is good."

Then, he decided to sing the song he felt on his heart. *Why do preachers want to sing all the time? Join the freakin' choir!*

He preached about forty-five minutes. I imagine I was the only timekeeper. I may have been in lala land for about the first ten minutes; however, I was drawn into the last thirty-five. He spoke about how no weapon formed against one would prosper.

He went on to say, "What God has for you is for you."

Pastor Samuels emphasized the devil came to "steal, kill, and destroy." I was beginning to feel that fire thing.

Before I knew it, I had stood up and was screaming, **"Say it! The devil is a liar! Amen!"**

Isaac didn't know how to respond. I had never stood up before. Believe it or not, I wasn't putting on. I was really feeling the sermon.

Then came the *um ya* and spitting up sounds preachers make before reaching the climax of their sermon. I used to laugh at them at that point. It was like they would start making beep bop noises, then they'd get choked on their own saliva. Then they would pull out their initialized handkerchief to violently spit in it in front of everyone. Finally, they would either pause in the middle of the moment to either sip on water or juice, or to take the time to put a cough drop in their mouth another pastor just so happened to have available. If I would have eaten breakfast before I came to church, I probably could have easily puked right in service. *Just gross!*

Anyway, Pastor Samuels spoke on how families must stick together. He emphasized, no one was perfect and reminded us of God's mercy. For a moment, I thought the entire service was a set up, but I was reminded of what my mother, Willie Mae, and others used to say.

72

They said, "Even the devil can preach the Word, so don't always tune into the messenger, but instead, listen to the message."

The older I became the more sense it made. Funny how things made sense umpteen years after it was said.

It was then I decided I was not going to let Quintella ruin my marriage. I felt we needed to find a new church home. My plan was to talk to Isaac even though I knew he'd go with the flow. He always did. God knew it wasn't meant for Rev. Dickerson or Queen B. to be in service. He also knew it *was* meant for Isaac and me to be in service. That's why God is good all the time. He saved me from making a fool out of myself. Sometimes I got it, other times I didn't.

On that note, I thanked Him. The Christian journey could be mighty challenging at times! I could hear Willie Mae singing, "Hang on my sista, change is gonna come."

For the invitation portion of church, Isaac grabbed me by the hand; we walked down for *special* prayer. Really, people are not supposed to go down for prayer during invitation, but they do. After we made it to the front, half of the church decided to follow. Pastor Samuels led everyone in prayer again. We stood there for eternity. I recall switching from leg to leg at least four times; I pulled my hand from Isaac at least twice to wipe off the moisture that had accumulated on my palms. *Black folk Baptist church!*

Finally, church was almost over. We returned to our seats, the choir sang one last song, and then the benediction was recited. I rushed to pick up the kids. I really didn't want to linger around, hug and kiss people, and hold long outdrawn conversations. Isaac trailed behind me. He must have been just as ready to go; he was on my heels. Another reason I didn't want to linger was because my feet were killing me! Women tend to put on what I call one-hour shoes—shoes meant to be worn for only one hour, or else your feet would feel like you had been walking on concrete all day.

Isaac decided it would be a nice afternoon to take the kids for ice-cream. For a moment I assumed he thought we were back under the same roof; but then he asked if I would be interested in having a little company later. He wanted to spend time with me and the kids. He said it would mean the world to him. Put on the spot, I said "sure." I am thinking I would have said sure regardless. I missed my chocolate drop!

Some sermons tend to make one feel convicted. I felt ashamed about my premeditated intentions of ruining service. I thanked God for everything that took place. He knew! Rev. Dickerson and his Pumpkin would have to answer to God. There was no reason for me to add myself to the list. I was sure Isaac felt bad enough for having the affair. There was no use throwing it up in his face all the time.

Willie Mae would say, "Forgive but don't forget."

There was also a saying, "If it happens once, shame on them. If it happens twice, shame on you."

After the confession, I genuinely believed it would never happen again. So, from that point on I planned to leave it at that. I guess you can say, I left my troubles at the altar.

Contemplating

No matter what goes on in life, I've learned that life goes on. Summer came as anticipated, so did fall. Daytime came when due, and so did nighttime. School was back in session: Isaac Jr., a fifth grader, JaRon a third grader, and Danielle a first grader. Danielle was nervous until she saw most of her friends were still in her class. JaRon, my little chopper, was excited because he had another opportunity to take up karate. If I had to give him a nickname, it would have been "Chopper" for sure. Isaac Jr. was ready to get fifth grade over with so he could graduate on to middle school.

The separation had not affected the kid's behavior at home or school. Isaac must have explained our little dilemma better than I credited him. The kids respected their teachers; they made good grades. No naughty calls regarding any of them. Isaac and I may have had our issues, but we stood together when it came to discipline. We left room for the kids to make mistakes, but at the same time, in the Singleton household, failure was not an option.

Though my title was Mrs., I considered myself a married, single, working mother. *I wonder if there are any greeting cards for that title.* I was a sista who had issues. One situation after another, whether big or small, there was always something to deal with, to do, or to decide. I would have had to be a fool to think life would be a bowl of cherries. I knew issues would arise. I guess I didn't know they would accumulate daily.

JaRon, with his karate chopping self, would say, "Roll with the chops, Mom."

I was rolling alright.

After our little church rendezvous, Isaac mentioned his six-month lease was approaching an end. He expressed desires to return home, though he was willing to sign another six-month lease if I needed additional time. Signing six months could have been another one of his smooth moves. Most leases were twelve months. We were seeing each other more frequently, but my feelings were not stable; deciding was mind-boggling.

One struggle was Isaac kept Shantel every Wednesday and every other weekend. My nerves advocated for me; they spoke up and said, "Not yet, Evette!" If I wanted my marriage to work, I was aware I had to accept that reality. *Ugh!* Another problem was my imagination; it was all over the place. I often wondered if Queen B. had been to the same places I had been. Hell, I wanted Isaac to get a new car just because I despised the fact she had been in my seat. The thought of *my* husband pulling down his pants to share his goodies with someone else was enough to make me puke. Bearing the pain had been worse than childbirth. Weird, but sometimes I wasn't sure if my pain was due to the affair itself, or because it was an affair with Quintella out of all people!

Did I not look better than her? Had our sex played out?

Dr. Gregg assured me that my thoughts were reasonable. She advised me to continue my Xanax.

Part of me wanted to wait another six months. Part of me wanted *my* boo back home. For goodness sake, we slept in the same bed for nine years! The kids missed him even though they hadn't expressed it. *Decisions, decisions!* Once again, another situation…. another decision left up to *me* to solve.

I wished Willie Mae were still around to provide wisdom. Usually, I could think of what she'd say if she were alive, but for the first time I wasn't too sure what she'd say. I could only assume she would have wanted me to stick to biblical principles and to work things out with Isaac. I knew my dad, Marlon, would have been open to advice. I'm sure he would have said, "I don't know what to tell you."

Those were his favorite words. His advice would have left me at square one.

Ultimately, Dr. Gregg was who I sought to convey all my deepest marital secrets. At least I could hold her accountable to maintain confidentiality. I shared bits and pieces with Ms. Joyce Ann; I knew she could relate. Other than that, I never told my co-workers, friends, or neighbors my business or ever ask for their opinions. Folk are quick to say what they'd do, when in fact they probably wouldn't take their own advice if faced with the same situation. If I hadn't learned anything over the years, I learned to at least pray and let God provide insight, or just make my own decisions based on my heart.

Sophia provided her unwelcomed two cents from time to time, but I ignored her unexperienced input. She assumed she had my undivided attention and I cared. When it boiled down to it, I didn't care or give a hoot about her opinions. I just nodded yes, said okay, and moved the hell on. I imagine she had good intentions; she was just clueless. As far as I was concerned, she walked in *her* flip flops with her heels sticking out, and not in *my* shoes.

Thank God Isaac was not the abusive type. Lord knows a coworker of mine was hit, kicked, choked, body slammed, and spit on by her ex-husband. Bless her heart, I thought I had problems. Which was worse? I could see myself walking away if Isaac treated me as such, but who knows? No doubt someone would have ended up in jail, or dead....it would not have been me! Cheating was a piece of cake when it came to other issues I heard about. *At least that was my justification.*

Isaac had his share of friends; they rarely met up. I never overheard him gossiping while around his friends or on the phone. Knowing him, he kept everything to himself and went about life as normal. *I wonder who he would have consulted if I had gotten pregnant by another man. Would he have kicked me out?* Thank God I'd been the faithful one. I didn't plot two years to get *my* dream man just to have an affair with someone else.

New Neighbor on the Block

I decided I needed another six months to get over the affair. I wanted to give Isaac a little bit longer to ponder about his shortcoming, while I continued to work on myself. I was not feeling some other woman's baby in the house yet. I figured I could always reevaluate in another six months. In the meantime, maybe I could develop a special love for baby Shantel.

It was different having a stepchild who came *with* the marriage, than having one who popped up *after* the fact. I didn't want to resent her; I did what was best for everyone. Plus, I knew by winter, Isaac could move back in, just in time to prevent all the pipes from freezing. And by then, maybe I'd be ready for him to keep me warm in a *good* way. We hadn't had sex since *dream night*. I wasn't feeling it either. I didn't care how sexy Isaac was, with his no wearing condom ass!

That's why I needed more time. I kept saying sarcastic shit.

Isaac respected my decision and signed another lease. He proposed for more family time instead of just having his moments with the kids. I acknowledged his proposal and suggested we spend at least every other Wednesday together. I knew he'd have Shantel. I figured I'd start off by seeing the little turd. Isaac was receptive of that idea. One thing for sure, I knew I was not going to be changing diapers and carrying her around. Not! This was just a Christian gesture to do the right thing, I needed more time for all of that. My days of diaper changing were over!

Quintella's name was barely brought up. Rev. Dickerson had been long out the picture. I had not been to church since that God saving Sunday, nor had Isaac. The kids had not been back since before summer camp. I considered looking for a new church home. Meanwhile, I watched T.D. Jakes and Joyce Meyers on television. They were so enlightening and uplifting. At one point, I considered not going back to physical church. There was nothing like folding clothes and cooking all at the same time while getting the Word. I didn't want to deprive the kids from church though. I figured our problems shouldn't affect them. They enjoyed going to church and being in the choir. So, my goal was to find a church with a choir that was led by a man, *and* a pastor who had no kids close to Isaac's age.

Life was complicated!

So many things to consider.

Knock. Knock.

The soft sound on my door brought me out of my reverie. I knew it was not Sophia; it was a gentler knock. I knew it was not Ms. Joyce Ann; she was in Atlanta in a fashion show competition, having her clothes modeled.

"Hello," I said as I reluctantly opened my door.

It was Gina, our newest neighbor down towards the end of the cul-de-sac. Or, you could say the beginning depending on your perspective, second house from the corner. Apparently, she was going door to door to introduce herself. She was a nice-looking lady, on the taller side, and slim. You could tell she worked out; she was wearing exercise attire.

"My name is Evette Singleton," I responded to her introduction, while disclosing I had three kids who were off to school, and I had a *husband* who was off to work.

She already knew Isaac! He was already on her *to do* list. To do list, meaning to cut her yard. She had previously stopped by Sophia's house, so Sophia had already informed her Isaac was *my* husband.

Gina claimed two kids. Her husband was in the military serving overseas. Reportedly, he had connections to help her and the kids get a house. They had been staying with family, which was becoming a problem. For her to not know me, she told me more than I cared to know.

85

I welcomed Gina to the neighborhood. I didn't know what else to say. When we had our home built, I didn't go around introducing myself. We bumped into everyone over time. Maybe she was looking for friends. Unfortunately, I was not looking for any new acquaintances. I was willing to be neighborly, but she could forget the friendship thing.

As she walked away, I noticed she had a tattoo on her left calf. Not to judge her from the start, but she didn't strike me as someone who would have a tattoo. She seemed prissier, like she was a princess or something; hard to explain. She just didn't appear to be the tattoo type. She reminded me of the brats back at Bakersville High. Isaac didn't care for prissier people back then. I figured the threat was minimal.

Not too long after Gina jogged down the street, Sophia trotted over. I mean it hadn't been five minutes!

Knock! Knock!

Yep, it was her pounding.

"Well, good evening," were her choice words of greeting.

I smirked; I knew she was coming to gossip about Gina.

"I see Gina just left," she felt the need to inform me of the known.

"Yes," I replied.

Sophia went on to say, "She's a cute little ole thang, isn't she?"

"Yes," I answered, trying not to feed into her tactics.

Then, she added, "She seems pretty nice. One thing about her is she's married."

Sophia chuckled after that comment. I decided I'd start up another topic to shut her instigating down.

"So, how do you think Ms. Joyce Ann is doing down in Atlanta?" I asked.

"I think she's making tons of money as usual," she went along with the change of subject.

Sophia knew me. She knew exactly why I switched the conversation. Ain't nobody got time for that all the time!

"I saw the little outfits Ms. Joyce Ann made. They were adorable as can be. I imagine she'll at least place," she went on to say.

No doubt Ms. Joyce Ann was doing her thing out there. She was a go-getter; a pure example of life going on.

"Well, I guess we will have to wait until she gets back. She has not called to provide an update," I added.

"Yep," Sophia concurred.

Shortly after that, Sophia decided to trot on back across the street. Her visits got shorter and shorter when I didn't let her get to me. Po lady, she didn't have anything better to do. She literally dressed up in her rainbow colors every day to do absolutely nothing. I don't know how she paid her bills. It was like she was there living for free. Her car didn't work. Majority of the time you'd see her wobbling to the mini-mart and back, pretty much her life in a nutshell. Funny how she loved jabbering on the phone but she never called me. She'd rather wobble over instead.

It was Isaac's day to stop by the school and pick up the kids. I was glad he had a key. Lord knows going to the door three times in one day had worn me out: Once for the mail, once for Gina, and once for Sophia. I hadn't been to the door that much in years. I knew with my luck; the kids would get out of the car and JaRon would come ring the doorbell, while Isaac made his walk around the yard to make sure everything was okay. So, I'd have to answer the door anyway. It was like people knew when to disturb; I could hang by the door all day; no knock-knock or ding-dong. Let a sista sit down and get comfortable— knock-knock, ding-dong.

Anytime Isaac stopped by, he'd go out of his way to make sure the house was okay. I didn't have to worry about any maintenance issues inside or out. He checked everything and fixed things before they became a problem. I swear I had Mr. Fixer Upper himself. Mr. Perfect.

How could Mr. Perfect make such a drastic mistake? Will I ever truly forgive him?

Church Visit

The kids and I had not been to church in about seven months. I had been eyeing one near my job. I decided the upcoming Sunday would be the best day to visit. The name of the church was Sky's the Limit Baptist Church. The pastor's name was Marquis Hill. My co-worker, LaShawn, convinced me to give it a try. I heard he was wonderful and inspiring. He had pastored the church for over ten years. From the get-go, I liked that he was married and had two teenaged children. Isaac may have fallen for a preacher's daughter; he would not fall for a teenager. He was gullible but not sick!

I figured I'd go alone initially. If I liked it, I would take the kids and then see if Isaac would accompany us. To my understanding, people wore jeans, t-shirts, and I heard some even wore shorts and flip flops. I grew up in a church where members dressed up like Sr. Geraldine Buckingham. There came a time when women could wear dressy pants. I was grateful for that because I only wore pants. If Willie Mae were around, she'd have a lecture over the dress code. The Bible points out to come as you are. If I expected change in my life, I needed to be receptive to change. *Why not?*

Sunday arrived; Isaac was over tending the lawn before the break of dawn. I allowed the kids to sleep in so they wouldn't ask fifty million questions. I informed Isaac I was headed to try out a new church; he didn't seem to mind. I asked if he knew anyone who attended. He denied. I couldn't say I trusted him 100% yet.

At church, I was immediately greeted by about five people before I reached my seat. *Whew*...I appreciated the kindness, but it did make me feel a little uneasy. I wasn't used to being greeted by more than one to two ushers at the door entrance. The church had greeters *and* ushers; something different for sure.

Service started at ten o'clock a.m. When I say ten o'clock, I mean it literally. I was waiting on the deacons to come out. Instead, a praise team skipped out while clapping their hands. At first, I thought I was attending a concert. The crowd was immediately pumped up and involved. I didn't know whether to throw my hands up in the air like I didn't care or what. Eventually everyone was welcomed. The praise team led about three songs before the assistant pastor came out and welcomed everyone again. Then, he prayed.

After prayer, a huge screen lowered from above. The praise team sang additional songs. Words were projected on the screen for the members to join along. Initially, I felt a little out of place, but the vibes from the people came across as authentic. Before I knew it, I was drawn into the vibes and was singing along. I finally stood up because only a few people were still seated, and they were elderly.

After the music selections, Pastor Hill leaped up the steps to the stage and welcomed everyone again. If anything, I felt welcomed. He prayed and immediately went into his sermon entitled, "If Jesus Was Wronged, What Makes You Think You Won't Be?"

Again, I felt the sermon was directed towards me. It was not the first time I had been to church and felt as though someone was speaking directly to me.

"God is omnipresent," I reminded myself.

The sermon was exactly what I needed. Even though it was the first time I visited Sky's the Limit Baptist Church, I knew it would be my new church home. No need for church hopping. I could already visualize the kids enjoying the service. They had kid's church as well. I could visualize Isaac enjoying the church too. There is a saying, "Mama knows best!" I knew. I hurried home to share my experience.

Isaac was outside talking to Gina!

The devil is a liar!

I assumed she was making her daily walk around the cul-de-sac and neighborhood and found it necessary to stop to talk to Isaac. I pulled up in the driveway, shifted the car in park, cut off the motor, and got out. I switched straight up to Isaac and gave him a big kiss on the cheek. He knew why. He went with the flow. I said hello to Gina, but in a less friendly voice.

"I sure hope she doesn't become an issue. Lord knows I refuse to let someone else mess up things further," I muttered under my breath.

Giving the situation the benefit of the doubt, I excused myself. I switched on in the house to see what the kids were up to, hoping they were out of bed and up moving around.

Isaac came in shortly afterwards. Supposedly Gina stopped by to remove herself from the *to do* list. Isaac said Gina's nephew moved in from Florida. She was going to buy a lawn mower and have him cut her grass.

"Good, I would hate to have to body slam a sista!" I responded.

Isaac popped me on the butt and giggled. He nodded his head as he went to freshen up. For him to visit from time to time, he freely went about the house the same as though he was back home.

Ask me if I really cared? No!

I found it charming. I wanted to go freshen up with him. Nothing sexier than seeing a man all hot and sweaty. I had to remind myself I had just gotten home from church.

Boy, it sho was easy to get distracted!

I checked on the kids. Danielle was still asleep. I woke her up. Isaac Jr. and JaRon were putting on their clothes for the day. I changed out of my church attire and headed straight to the kitchen to prepare dinner like the mom of the year, hoping to be rewarded by Isaac's company for dinner.

As I was chopping onions for my smothered liver and onion dinner, Isaac slipped behind me and began nibbling on the back of my neck. I must have jumped so hard. I almost chopped off my index finger! I managed to keep my composure. He made a sista want to strip naked in the kitchen. I twirled around and gently pushed Isaac back.

"Be good!" I said in my playful voice.

Isaac grinned. He said he was sorry; he didn't mean to startle me or step out of line.

To regain normalcy, I asked Isaac if he would be available and interested in attending church the following Sunday, assuring him I was aware he'd have Shantel. Fascinated by yet another one of my kind gestures, Isaac said, "I can definitely make that happen."

I asked if he'd stay for dinner.

Once again, he responded, "I can definitely make that happen."

I wanted to ask if he could stay the entire freakin' night, but I had to snap out of my hormonal moment. I had a feeling he would have responded he could definitely make that happen too.

For the first time in a long time, I didn't have an angry moment being around Isaac. No thoughts of Quintella. No resentment when I mentioned Shantel. Nothing Isaac did irked me. I was beginning to see light at the end of the tunnel.

It was about darn time!

Moving Forward

Seven days of waiting seemed like eternity. Apart from one family addition, the Singleton family church day had arrived. I felt vibrant! I was happy! I anticipated a great day. The kids and I impatiently waited for Isaac *and* Shantel. We were ready for church. Isaac asked if he could drive over with Shantel, then take my SUV. Yet another potential smooth move; I did not mind his suggestion. I was cool with that.

Honk! Honk!

"Dad and Shantel are here!" I shouted to the kids; forgetful we were all in the same room.

All three sprinted out the door, full of excitement, thrilled to see their half-sister more than anything.

I briefly prayed, "Lord, help me stay strong. What is done is done. Please help me be loving to Shantel. Remind me that she's innocent. Amen."

While Isaac removed the car seat from his car, I backed the SUV out of the garage. Isaac opened the door to the back seat to position Shantel in the car. I hurriedly shifted the car in park, opened my door and leaped to the other side.

"I will fasten her, let me see the little angel." I made an effort to demonstrate courtesy.

Isaac was caught off guard by my kind-heartedness. I sensed it took a lot of weight off his shoulders. No telling what had gone through his head on his way over. I had never seen Shantel in person. I figured there was no better time. It was bound to happen one day.

I buckled in Shantel. She was a beautiful little girl. She had a look of innocence in her big bright eyes; awake as could be. The kids jumped in their designated spots, buckled up, and Isaac took over the driver's side. We were off to church.

Of course, Sophia was sitting out on the porch, looking over her red-rimmed glasses as though she couldn't see through the lens itself. I waved and rolled my eyes at the same time. In my head I couldn't help but think she'd be knocking on my door at the first opportunity.

Isaac overjoyed, extended his hand for my hand. Talking about chills down a sista's spine. Boy, did I miss that! Shantel and the kids were quiet all the way. All smiles.

We attended service together our first time. Shantel was not my biological daughter, but I never have grasped why people send their kids to children's class not knowing much about the people or the church. I had good vibes, but… I wanted to attend a few more times and at least visit the children's classes first. That was just my nature.

The kids were intrigued by the new environment. Shantel whined a little bit, babbled here and there, but for the most part, she was good. By the time Pastor Hill began his sermon, Shantel was out like a light.

What is it about preaching that puts kids to sleep?

His sermon was titled, "Taking it One Day at a Time." Once again, too weird for words. Coincidental. The kids were on their best behavior. Isaac and I were able to tune in to the Word.

After the sermon, Isaac whispered, "This is really nice."

He spoke highly of the people. He felt the authenticity. I did not share that before; nice to see we had mutual feelings. There were also greeters stationed in the parking lot. Isaac ended up talking to some guy for a while. In the meantime, I fastened Shantel in her seat again. I peeped in her diaper. It was dry. I thanked God. I still wasn't feeling the diaper change thing.

Isaac eventually freed himself from conversation. Apparently, the greeter had seen Isaac in his neighborhood cutting grass. His name was Benjamin Michael.

"How about that, two first names," I felt the need to point out.

Benjamin asked Isaac if he could use help. He explained he was laid off his job and had a baby on the way. Isaac had taken his number. He told Benjamin he may be able to find something for him to do. I found that odd, being that he liked to do his own work. He always did everything by himself. Weird moments were on the rise. All I could do was continue to roll with the chops.

On the way home, JaRon asked out of the blue, "Can we go to the buffet for dinner?"

He liked to fix his own plate so he could get what he wanted, and then go back for ice-cream and candy. Isaac Jr. and Danielle decided to join in on the request. Funny, little Shantel had awakened and made a sound as though she was trying to put in her two cents. We went to Bob's Buffet. It had been at least a year since we had been to a buffet as a family. Now we were going as an extended family. I didn't know what to think. I just kept riding it out.

There was no wait to be seated. Normally on Sundays there was at least a twenty-minute wait. We were seated next to the buffet, which made it easier to keep an eye on the kids. I took the honor of taking Shantel and relieving her from her car seat. When I checked her diaper, she was wet *and* dirty. Without thinking twice, I reached for her diaper bag and carried her to the ladies' room. Somehow, she was beginning to grow on me. She was a calm baby. She didn't favor Quintella as much as I thought. All I needed was to see Quintella in her, I probably would have dropped her. Imagine having to explain

100

that! She had Isaac's nose and beady eyes. A baby with a Pinocchio nose would have been so not fair.

Poor Isaac didn't know what to think. He seemed shocked every time I embraced caring for Shantel. He loved her. The kids loved her. I figured I might as well start loving her. I returned to the table. The kids were already seated with their food. Isaac had fixed his plate and mine, and he had Shantel's bottle ready to go. It looked like cereal was added to the formula. Praise the Lord she was not on breast milk. I understood breast milk was best, but not when it was not your child.

Uh, that would have been gross!

JaRon led us in prayer before we dug in. Isaac took on his responsibility to feed Shantel before eating his own food. He instructed me to go ahead and eat. So, I did! I was cool with that.

Moments later, the waiter seated our fellow table neighbor just to our left. It was Benjamin Michael. He was alone. Strange, he ended up next to us. For him to be in search of extra money, he had money to eat out. Not to say broke people couldn't eat out, but it did trigger a little thought.

Benjamin should have been seated with us, for the remainder of dinner, he was all up in our family time. Somewhat annoyed, I tried not to let it interfere with the joy I felt for the first time in a long time. While Isaac and Benjamin yakked on and on about yard work, I focused in on the kids. I asked if they liked church. They all said, "Yes ma'am" at the same time. It was nice to know they enjoyed it. They had no clue what children's church would be like.

Isaac's conversation with Benjamin started to dwindle down. The kids were full off junk food. Shantel babbled from contentment. I was full.

"Honey are you ready to go?" I asked.

"Yes, I would say that I am," Isaac replied.

Isaac introduced Benjamin, which was a little backwards. We had only been there almost an hour; he introduced us at the end. Isaac shook Benjamin's hand. He mentioned, "I'll see you tomorrow."

Back in the car, I asked Isaac what he meant about seeing Benjamin. He agreed to give him a little work to help him out. According to Isaac, his lawn business was getting to be more than he could handle; he had about five additional yards. I never understood why he didn't seek help from the start. I understood independent work as a black man; I didn't understand independently working. Isaac either had a change of heart and was seeing things in a new perspective, or, he had finally come to his senses.

According to Isaac's and Quintella's personal agreement, Isaac had to have Shantel back home by three o'clock p.m. on Sundays. He needed to get us home to switch cars. I was cool with that; plus, I didn't have a choice. I was exhausted anyway. I figured I could get home, help the kids find something constructive to do, and maybe I could take a nap.

Isaac pulled up in the driveway; and he got out. I walked around to the driver's seat so I could put the SUV back in the garage. We hugged one another. I received a big juicy kiss on the lips. Short but sweet. Sweet enough that chills shot down my spine and my vaginal lips squeezed together and released. Isaac kissed the kids, including the boys. He was a firm believer in fathers kissing their boys. It was something his father always did. The kids kissed Shantel on her little cheeks, who was crying for the first time as though she didn't want the day to end. I walked back around and kissed Shantel on her forehead. Isaac fastened Shantel into the back seat of the BMW, got in on his side and blew me a kiss. I'd say there was so much kissing going on in the family you would have thought someone had returned home after years of being away. Lovely day!

Run in with an Old Classmate

Monday morning. Sophia was up bright and early, sitting on the porch in rainbow fashion, flapping her jaws on the phone. For the first time ever, I wondered who on earth did she talk to! Was it the same person? Different people? I was sure the day would come for me to be enlightened.

Gina was out and about making her stroll around the circle. She had a little white poodle looking dog with her; the first time I had seen her walking a dog.

"Hey Gina!" I made an effort to speak first.

"Hey there, how are you?" she responded, still in motion.

"I am blessed and highly favored," I replied, imitating how Sophia would have sounded.

Gina kept on strolling. Apparently, she was on a mission. I had to give her props for her consistency. Lord knows I needed to exercise; I could never fit it in my schedule. My life was exercise by itself. As stressed as I had been, I had already lost weight.

It was a great day to restock on groceries. The weather was in its cooperative state. The food selection was scarce, and I felt as though I'd be fixing Isaac a plate more routinely. I made a dash to the mailbox while Sophia jabbered on the phone; what better time to avoid conversation.

"Hey sweetie!" she hollered anyway.

I threw up my hand, walking as though I was in a hurry. I was in a hurry alright; a hurry to get to my car. Thank God she was jabbering with someone else. I knew she had to be dying to know what was going on with Isaac and me. I didn't have fifteen minutes to spare. As I sped out the driveway, I glanced over at Ms. Joyce Ann's. No signs she had returned.

Grocery shopping was my least favorite. The Bargain Saver was ten minutes away. The store was always crowded, people carried on like the store was going out of business. You'd think it was Black Friday every day, but at a grocery store instead of a department store or mall. Customer service sucked; management obviously didn't enforce professionalism. There was a Cornelius' Groceries about thirty minutes away. It was a nicer store and was family owned. Customer service was superb! Ten minutes; however, was distant enough.

"Well, well, well... *Evette*," a voice said behind me as I grabbed my basket; some people would say cart. I spun around to the face of Michelle Lee, who I knocked down in high school for giving *my* Boo Bear water from her sports bottle.

"W-well, h-hey, th-there," I stuttered from disbelief. "L-long, ti-time, no, s-ee," I stuttered on.

"Yeah it's been some time," she validated. "How often do you shop here?" she questioned.

"As little as possible," I was finally able to say without stuttering. "I hate coming to the store," I added.

Michelle Lee claimed she came to the store no less than every few days.

"How have you been?" I initiated the next question so I could have more control of the conversation.

"I have been wonderful," she responded.

She expressed how happy she was to see me and complimented me on how good I looked.

Michelle Lee, with no shame in her game, asked if Isaac and I were still kicking it. Assuming she did not know my business, I said, "Girl yes, of course...you know he was *my* Boo Bear back in the day."

"Um hmm, I remember oh too well," she mumbled.

Without me asking, she made sure to mention she was happy, had a stepdaughter, and she was expecting a child. I congratulated her as I started to advance my basket, ready to get on with my shopping.

"Nice seeing you," I said.

"Same here," she responded.

I assumed she must had forgiven me for knocking her big butt down back in the day. Speaking of big butt, she had lost quite a bit of weight. As a matter of fact, the girl looked good; she seemed altogether different. People do change…I guess I was the aggressive one back then. I couldn't imagine I'd be the same over a knuckle head. Then again, who knows…. Isaac was one of a kind. *My man!*

I gathered my groceries and headed toward the check out, hoping Michelle Lee had already parted way. It was odd speaking to her, and a little strange she frequented the store and I had not run into her. Seeing her brought flashbacks to Quintella. Lord knows I was doing my best to wean her out of my mind. They were best friends; it was hard not to think of both when seeing one.

At least I had on decent clothes. Usually I'd throw on sweats to go to the store. I took the time to put on presentable clothes and a little make-up. Nothing like seeing someone you had not seen in years; they look decent and you don't. I wondered if she was married. She just said she was pregnant. I also wondered if she really had a stepdaughter. She was a habitual liar back in the day. I did not see a ring on her finger. In my opinion, she did not look like she was expecting. One thing I did know was she didn't have to be married to get pregnant. Oh well, I still had Isaac. If she didn't get anything else out of our conversation, I bet she got that!

Leaving my grocery experience behind, I decided to drive around to see if I could locate Isaac cutting grass, a typical routine of mine. Isaac didn't mind. I made a turn down Camille Avenue and swung a right onto 52nd Street. Yep, there they were, Isaac and Benjamin working away at the second house from the corner. No intent to disturb them, I blew my horn and kept going. Isaac turned and waved. Benjamin kept about his work as though he did not hear my horn. I was cool with that. I was only speaking to *my* boo anyway.

I didn't recall the house being one of Isaac's routine customers. Trust me, I was familiar with his routine. I had a visual of all his residences. The house was brick with maroon trimming. There was a big tree in the middle of the yard with a bed of rocks encircling the tree. There were a few baby items on the porch and a kiddie pool by the steps of the porch. Yep, you better believe a sista saw all that in five seconds while going fifteen miles per hour. I added the house to my visual. I kept up with everything more than ever. I hated to be that way, but Isaac brought it on himself.

As I entered the driveway, I was not surprised to see Sophia still on the phone jabbering away. *Sophia.... that lady!* There was a van in Ms. Joyce Ann's driveway. She flew to Atlanta. I was not sure whose

109

van it could be. She never got rentals. I just assumed she had made it back home safely. In due time, I would find out the scoop either directly from her or Sophia. I pulled into the garage, allowed the door to close before exiting my SUV. I left enough room to grab my groceries from the back.

A Call from Baby's Mama

As much as I hated dragging bags of groceries in the house, I had to anyway. The kids were in school. Even if they were home, Danielle, bless her heart, could only carry in one bag at a time. JaRon had excuses; he acted like the lightest bag was the heaviest. Isaac Jr. would carry in at least two. Overall, I ended up carrying the majority. Then, I was always the one stuck putting up all the groceries.

By the time I made five trips back and forth from the kitchen to the car, ten minutes had gone by. The sackers always put four to six items in each bag, leaving customers to carry about twenty. Before I could put away the groceries, I was worn out from bringing them in. I had to put them up right away; things could spoil. The sackers at Bargain Saver were not trained on how to bag groceries; there would be bars of soap in with the bread, and laundry detergent in with the meat. Some days I would speak my mind; some days I would just do my best to hurry home to separate everything. *Who wanted their salami sandwich to taste like Gain detergent?*

As I put my last can of Green Giant French Style Green Beans in the cupboard, the phone rang.

Who on earth could be calling the house phone?

We hardly used the house phone. We only used it to call our cell phones when we misplaced them. We figured it would be nice to keep a landline as back up in case there was an emergency.

It was a local, but unfamiliar number. I wasn't going to pick up, but curiosity got the best of me. In a disguised voice, I answered,

"Hello."

There was about a three second pause before the caller said, "Hello *Evette,*" as though she was saying hello and asking if it was me at the same time.

No doubt it was a female.

"This is she," I replied in my normal voice.

Another three seconds…*what's up with all the pauses?*

"This is Quintella."

My heartbeat sped up a notch.

"Why is this bitch calling me?" I thought to myself.

112

I remained silent to see if she'd say anything else.

Quintella went on to say she hated to call; she needed to get in touch with Isaac. He had not answered *her* calls nor responded to *her* texts over the last several days. She claimed to have gotten the house number out of the church directory. Whatever she wanted sounded urgent. I didn't care!

How is she going to call a sista and think imma be her message relater? Her trifling ass never bothered to apologize. Hell to the no!

"Excuse me!" I said, my voice raising. **"You think you can call here and tell me you are trying to reach *my* husband after you tricked him into getting you pregnant! You have never bothered to apologize to me! You must be out of your cotton-picking mind to think I could possibly care about your damn needs right now!"**

Honestly, I knew she had to be calling for something related to Shantel, but so what? She was wrong. I had been doing good all this time. No Xanax in days. Knowing she was on the other line was all it took to shift me back into *imma beat yo ass* mode! Caught up in the moment, I continued to vent,

"And your conniving ass wanna be a preacher dad was the one who started all this mess! What is so freakin' urgent that you are calling *my* house to hunt down Isaac?"

Quintella had the nerve to say she had been *notified* Isaac had not called to speak to Shantel in the last several days. He always called her to say goodnight. She wanted to make sure that he was okay.

Please tell me the stupid girl didn't call about that! What did she mean she had been notified? Notified by who?!

I had to swallow my saliva before I could respond to such bull.

I mustered up enough energy before I could speak again,

"Girl, as long as your nose is long enough to reach the moon, don't ever call over here asking why *my* man ain't called to say goodnight! You better be glad he is man enough to keep her on his assigned days and he pays his fair share of child support. If you ever call here again, it better be because there is a life or death situation going on! Isaac doesn't stay here so don't call here, Bitch!"

The Lord must have been unpleased, I got a sudden itch in my throat and was coughing so hard I could no longer speak.

Quintella snickered and responded, "Whatever girl, I see you are still a trip."

She hung up in my face! If I had known where she stayed! I never purchased a church directory. All I knew was she stayed behind Rev. Dickerson. *The nerve of her!*

I called Isaac within seconds. Funny, he answered for me. Goes to show he knew who to answer to. I explained what had happened. He wasn't too enthused about any of it. Just when I had returned to my cloud nine stages, I was right back at square one. *What did she mean, that she had been notified?*

"All I know is she better not call here again for something like that!" I yelled to Isaac.

I didn't want to get mad at him. I wished he would have at least spoken up!

"Next time the hoochie might want to wait to see if you are going to pick up Shantel on Wednesday or your weekend and talk to you about her concerns then. Let her call again!" I threatened.

I had never foreseen myself speaking to someone else's mother so badly, but that girl hit a nerve. Every now and then I forgot I was a Christian. How Jesus was able to turn the other cheek was hard to comprehend. It proved He was the toughest person to walk the face of this earth!

Meanwhile, I poured a glass of wine. I hadn't had a drink in months; it was not advised with the Xanax. I plopped down on the living room sofa. If I were a smoker, that could have very well been a cigarette moment. I drank my wine until my nerves calmed. Quintella wasn't worth me using my prescription meds. *Skank! Ugh!*

"Precious Lord take my hand. Forgive me. Amen." I prayed.

115

A Mental Day Off: Visit to Neighbors

Tuesday and Wednesday went by peacefully. Thursday, yet another day. There had been activity at Ms. Joyce Ann's, but I had not seen her for several days; I was concerned that I hadn't physically laid my eyes on her. She would have at least dropped by. Whoever was in her house was not passing out any candies to the kids. I decided I'd pull a Sophia and go pay her a visit. My reasoning was more valid; it was based off suspicion. The van had come and gone, but the suspect was never witnessed.

Sophia was not sitting on the porch. Her front door was open, a sign she'd be out soon. I moseyed over to Ms. Joyce Ann's before Sophia came out. I couldn't wait to hear about her trip and her winnings. I knew she placed; she always did.

Before I could knock on the door, a young man answered. If I took a guess, I'd say a teenager. I introduced myself and asked if Ms. Joyce Ann was home.

"Hello, my name is Tré. Joyce is in Atlanta," he said.

Joyce? Who says Joyce?

I guess that explained the van and why I hadn't seen her.

"Is everything okay?" I asked.

"Yes, ma'am," he respectfully replied.

"Not to be rude or nosey, but who are you?" I aimed to comprehend the matter.

"I am Jerry's son." he responded.

Jerry was Ms. Joyce Ann's ex-husband. I was totally lost. Tré mentioned Jerry was in a nursing home in Atlanta, and "Joyce" was trying to locate him.

What did he mean by she was trying to locate him? Did he not know where he was?

He said Jerry had been diagnosed with pancreatic cancer and only had about six months to live.

I stood there perplexed. Jerry left Ms. Joyce Ann for a younger woman and he did relocate to Atlanta. For Tré to be a teenager, it revealed Jerry had been out there still getting his freak on, having children he couldn't have with Ms. Joyce Ann. *Player!* As much as I wanted to ask the whereabouts of his mother, unlike Sophia, I knew my limits.

I never wished anything bad on anyone except Quintella. I was a firm believer in karma. Evidently, karma had caught up with Jerry. His son seemed to be a decent young man; however, it didn't make a lick of sense for him to be in Ms. Joyce Ann's house. If anyone was ever left hanging, it was always me. I asked Tré to tell "Joyce" to call me and I moseyed on back next door.

Sophia had made it to her destination before I could sneak back into the house. I decided to swing on across the street to get whatever conversation she had pending out of the way. I knew the day would eventually come.

First, she inquired about what was going on at Ms. Joyce Ann's house. I shared everything Tré had mentioned, but in a non-gossiping way. Like I mentioned, Sophia was the neighborhood watch person, so I wanted her in the loop. Since Tré was a *foreign* person to the neighborhood, I figured she at least deserved to know that much.

Sophia inquired about Tre's mother. Coincidently, we thought the same thing. I told her I did not know anything about his mother. I left it at that. I was not going to get into any gossip. I had much respect for Ms. Joyce Ann. I would never speak of her or any situation involving her in a negative way.

119

Sophia sensed the conversation had come to a dead end. She decided to strike up a new conversation; the one I'd been waiting for. She inquired about Isaac and me. Privacy was not in her character. She was a bold sista all the way. She pointed out how she had seen the baby over a few times, and how she had seen us going back and forth to church. It didn't matter that we snuck in and out of the garage, Sophia had seen snippets, that was just enough for her. I explained we were working on things and I was trying my best to accept the situation and move forward. I did add we had a long way to go and we were taking it one day at a time.

Perfect timing, Isaac pulled up with the kids. So, I wrapped things up with Sophia just before she could get into the nitty gritty of our love story.

"Speaking of the devil, let me get my tail home so I can see how the kids' day went and what Isaac's plans are for the day." I excused myself.

"Girl you go ahead. I ain't mad at you, uh, don't let nobody keep you from your man chile," she felt the need to share her thoughts.

I smirked, turned around, and scurried back across the street.

Time had flown. More than likely it was because I had been on the move. I was down to working one day a week, more spare time at hand. I figured if I decided to let Isaac move back in, I'd quit. The house had been paid off for years. Isaac pretty much took care of everything. I liked that life better. He still paid the utilities even though he was not home. He promised he would continue to pay them as he did before he goofed up. I was cool with that. So, I just made luxury money for personal shopping.

Everyone was good. The kids updated me on their school day, which was basically what they had for lunch and what they did in extra curriculars. They never had homework. It was not a requirement. I had little educational games for them around the house and they each had a tablet. In their downtime on the weekend, they had obligations to spend at least thirty minutes twice a day working on educational assignments. Isaac and I agreed a little *home* work was reasonable.

Isaac was on the go. Some days he would hang around and other days he had work to accomplish. He had one more yard to cut for the day. He said he wanted to be back at the apartment before the maintenance crew arrived. Somehow, there was a leak coming from the ceiling tiles in his kitchen. He assumed the tenants above him had a big spill of some sort. So…there were his plans for the evening. I figured I would make some tacos and some Spanish rice for the kids and call it a day.

Visit to My All Star American

Once again, I had an increased need for some *chocolate affection*. I couldn't get enough. Sex had been out the picture; but having a little bit of chocolate handy was just as pleasurable. I craved Isaac's presence. I missed the smell of his Cool Water cologne and the sound of his baritone voice. My spine was having chill withdrawals. I had maintained well, but every now and then an empty feeling came over me. It wasn't the same, Isaac and I shared a bed for nine years. There I was all alone in our king-sized sleigh bed. No sleep lost, however, there were nights I longed to have his warm, smooth, soft skin up against my cool skin. I missed his special piece poking up against my lower back. Crazy me, I even missed his obnoxious snoring.

It had been eight months since Isaac got his apartment. I never visited, was tempted to drive by, but it was a gated community. I didn't have the code to enter, though I had hinted to Isaac several times. Typical of him, he didn't grasp my hints. *Are men really that clueless when it comes to hints?*

After Isaac's visit with the kids, I told him I wanted to check out his place. Of course, he was down; he said, "Anytime" and provided the gate code.

Since the opportunity was convenient, I decided to swing by. Why not? The kids were in school. It was not my one day to work. I pulled up to the gate, another car had just entered. I was tempted to speed through before the gate closed, but then I wouldn't have had the privilege of entering the code. A sista had to make sure it was legit. I entered 1 4 3 9, the gate didn't open.

What the hell? I know he didn't give me the wrong code!

Recalling back when I stayed in an apartment as a child, I figured I'd try once more and follow up with the pound sign. 1 4 3 9 # worked. Lord knows, I was about to call him and curse him out.

I drove down to the end of the second row, passing over several speed bumps. I made a right near the leasing office, and then took a left, followed by a right, before I saw the old Ford truck and BMW parked out in front of apartment 1577.

How would a robber make an escape with so many twists and turns? I guess he or she would have to scope the place out first.

For it to be an upscale apartment complex, I wasn't sure why there was no covered parking. One hailstorm and the BMW would have gotten jacked up!

It was a lovely day; a quiet environment; however, no sight of an animal, or human being. No Sophia's? *Are there any nosey people in apartment complexes, or is it just in housing editions?*

I thought about calling Isaac to make my arrival known. Instead, I decided to get out and knock on the door. His apartment was the only one lacking some kind of welcome mat. No decorations on the door, none in the window. *Poor man!* Maybe he was the only man in his section.

I tapped on the door using just my nails. Isaac opened the door within seconds. My boo had on some plaid shorts and what people call a wife beater tank top. I had no clue where that name came from. I just knew Isaac had never beaten me. He hardly wore shorts. He'd occasionally wear a tank top to bed with pajama pants or boxers.

I was greeted with a quick smack on the lips and escorted in. One tan sofa chair was noted in the living room with what looked like a 40-inch TV. There was an end table made of cherry wood next to the sofa and a medium sized, round multi-colored rug on the floor. It blended in with what little furniture he had. Though the living room was basically empty, the furniture was exquisite. The only time Isaac failed when it came to taste was when it came to Quintella, with her

Pinocchio nosed self; nose so long a tissue could get stuck up in there! *Ugh!*

Isaac offered me a drink and to sit if I pleased. Instead, I offered myself a tour of his apartment.

"Nah buddy, I gotta check this place out!" I insisted.

"Sure. My apartment is your apartment." Isaac said, ushering me to go ahead.

No time wasted, I passed the bathroom, peeked in, sniffed around for any unfamiliar scents. It was bare; he had a plain gray shower curtain up and a gray and white striped bath towel thrown over the curtain and a second towel on the floor. Maybe he was using it as a rug. I witnessed a few toiletries on the sink. Moving along, I entered his bedroom…the last room left to enter other than the kitchen. He had a one-bedroom apartment. There was a San Francisco 49ers bedspread on his bed. His bed was full-sized. He didn't pursue football, but he was a 49ers fan. Nothing about his apartment resembled our house. Let a man decorate and that is what you get.

I sniffed around in the bedroom too; a little harder than I did the bathroom. I peeked in the closet and opened a few dresser drawers. He had one tall dresser, and the end table that coordinated with the one in the living room. He had an ironing board up. His apartment was bare. What little he had, was in place.

As I made my way back to the kitchen, Isaac asked, "How was the inspection?"

He knew me!

"It was okay, I guess," I replied.

I tried to fight the temptation to bring up Quintella, but I just couldn't hold it in.

"Has Queen B. been over?"

Isaac claimed she had been in the front door long enough to pick up Shantel a few times; she had never sat down or been any further. I believed *my* Boo Bear. On that note, I felt comfortable enough to sit down.

Isaac made himself some coffee and joined me in the living room. He didn't have anywhere else to sit unless he sat on the floor. After we updated each other on how things had been; there were brief moments of silence. Odd, I felt like a shy girl on her first date who decided it was okay to visit someone's residence on the same day.

Three minutes passed, Isaac asked how things were looking for him to move back home. He had four months left of his second term.

"I imagine things are looking pretty good." I responded, trying not to sound excited.

I had thought about it beforehand, so it was not like I needed to contemplate any longer.

"Things may be a little rough, but I believe I'm ready to give it a try." I added.

Hell, I needed my man home for winter. I had been hard core long enough.

Isaac said he'd put in his thirty-day notice when the time came. He expressed how he appreciated me hanging in there, and he assured me he was terribly sorry for all he had put me through.

I looked at *my b*oo. I smiled. My body took control over me; I leaned in to give my first tongue kiss since the separation. Chills shot down my spine, my heart raced, my vagina lips pulsated waiting for Isaac's entry. Isaac gently leaned me back on the arm of the couch; he kissed me with such passion. I could feel his piece rising as my hormones continued to go haywire. His hands eased up my shirt and began caressing my breasts. Talking about a sista getting wet. "Poor couch" was all I could think. I knew the wetness had soaked through my little high-rise panties and through my denim mini skirt.

I knew what I was doing with the skirt.

Isaac stopped kissing me as though he was backing off for air, and he stopped caressing my breast.

What the hell?

128

Then…he stood up, scooped me up like a husband scoops his wife pridefully exiting the wedding chapel, and carried me to the bedroom where he gently landed me down on his bed. We ripped off each other's clothes. A sista needed that moment and was down one hundred percent! *My* sexy chocolate was all over me, satisfying my needs from head to toe. He slowly slid his penis into my soaking vagina. It was on!

Two minutes later, Isaac reached his climax. I was cool with that because I had reached mine too. It had been so long; I would have been pissed if he had lasted too much longer.

"Girl, you had no clue how bad I've wanted you! I hope you're okay with what just happened. Sorry baby, I had to have you. I couldn't wait any longer," Isaac pleaded.

"Honey it was all good. I miss you so much. I needed this," I assured.

We laid there in la la land for about fifteen minutes. I couldn't move. My climax had come and gone, but my body had not recuperated. My legs continued to shiver. I didn't know if I'd be able to walk. I was literally afraid to get up.

"Boo, you may have to help a sista get up," I said.

We laughed our hearts out. Oh, did we both need a good laugh!

"I guess you can say I finally helped you break in your apartment," I said while in a playful mood.

"Now that, you did," Isaac replied, managing to get up to grab a warm wet towel.

He gently wiped off my vagina, then gave me the towel to wipe off his shriveled-up penis, our normal routine after intimacy. It felt so good to do something normal. He jokingly said I could leave my panties if I wanted. Hell, I called his bluff. I put on my little mini skirt, buttoned up my blouse, and left my panties right on the floor where they ended. I knew he was kidding me, but I could tell he was thrilled I did.

In return for my panties, I resorted back to our high school days and asked Isaac if he had a shirt for me to sleep in. I wanted something with his scent to cuddle up in for my alone moments. I used to wear his jersey back in the day. Wearing his jersey made me feel on top of the world. In that moment, I felt on top of the world. *I love that man! Ugh...he better not mess up ever again! I will kill him!*

Back at the House

Eleven months had gone by. Isaac put in his thirty-day notice. My new mission was house cleaning. Isaac had been over a hundred times, but I wanted the house to be spic and span before he returned. Not only did my Boo Bear like expensive things, but also, he liked a spotless house. Not sure where he got that trait; at least it was a good one. Being that we married right out of high school, I never lived with another man other than my dad, Marlon Sampson. He wasn't necessarily who I'd call a neat freak. Willie Mae was left to do all the cleaning. There were days the house would be spic and span, and then days when the house could stand a little tidying. My dad wasn't bothered either way.

Speaking of my dad, he was alive and well. He was the grandpa Isaac Jr. imitated, the picture guy. Like Jr., dad packed his camera everywhere he went. He took pictures of people eating, dancing, sleeping, you name it. When I say pictures, I mean all sorts! No such thing as someone posing… just pictures of everyone doing anything at any time. He also took pictures of animals and nature, anything you can name. Ever since he retired as a machinist, photography had been his life.

The kids saw their grandpa from time to time. He lived about one hundred twenty miles away. He was what Willie Mae referred to as a "busy body;" pretty darn hard to catch. The kids called and texted him often. I was amazed how the older generation kept up with technology better than the younger generation. He responded to the kids using emojis and GIFs…it cracked me up. I wondered how he made it back then. It was like he was making up for lost time, keeping up with the Joneses.

Anyhow, I started off cleaning the bedroom; it could stand a little dusting. Basically, all I needed to do throughout the house was dust. If a plant could grow with dust instead of dirt, there would have been a flowerpot in every room. Understanding dust formation was something I never grasped.

Sophia had been on my mind lately, I reckoned it was about time to let her in on Isaac's upcoming return. If I ever wanted to get a message to the neighbors, I'd tell Sophia, sit back, and give it a day or two. She never let me down. If spreading gossip was a job, she'd be one rich lady. Maybe then she could get a pedicure and get those feet straightened up. *Lord have mercy on her feet!*

I heard a noise outside. I put my chores on halt as I rushed to see what was going on. Ms. Joyce Ann had pulled up. Boy was it nice to see her return! I decided not to bother her. I believe in letting people breathe a little bit before bombarding them. I was sure she'd come talk to me whenever she got settled. She looked great! She must have had a lot on her plate being that Tré was there.

"Thank You Lord for allowing Ms. Joyce Ann to return. Amen," I gave the Lord due praise.

In the meantime, back to housecleaning, but not without reminiscing about my love making episode. HBO didn't have anything on us. Seeing our bed distracted a sista. I can't emphasize enough how much I needed sex from my husband. Toys and other objects didn't quite do the trick. Like the song implied, there ain't nothing like having the real thing. I needed the real thing. *My* Boo Bear delivered! *Halleluiah!* I wanted to call him so badly to say get over here and give me some more. Ooh wee, damn, that was some good stuff! *What would the next time be like? Would it be every time from now on?*

Oh my, I was going crazy. I took a Xanax for my hormonal nerves, not sure it was meant for that, but something had to relax them. I had cleaning to do!

The kids were thrilled. I needed to know if Isaac planned to purchase Shantel a crib for her nights over. I didn't see one at his apartment. Trust me, there was none there. Surely, he knew she couldn't sleep in the bed. He knew that from when we had our kids.

Where would she sleep? Would she sleep in our room, or Danielle's?

133

I assumed she could sleep in Danielle's room and we could invest in a monitor. Danielle would be delighted to have company; she'd be a big sister for once.

Thoughts were floating in my mind. I had always been one who focused on the broader picture; by no means was I narrow-minded. Isaac was the neat freak. I was the planner. Put it this way, where he was weak, I was strong. That is what made us a compatible couple. My dad used to say, "Opposites attract." I'd agree. It was still mighty hard to believe Isaac slipped up. I finally had forgiven him. I had not forgotten. *How could I?!* All it took was a little sex. How about that!

Catching Up

Knock. Knock.

If a door were only good for about ten thousand knocks, we'd be getting a new one. It had to be Ms. Joyce Ann. It didn't sound like the knock I recalled from Gina, and of course it wasn't Sophia's.

"Hey lady, I am so glad to see you!" I shouted at Ms. Joyce Ann.

"Yeah girl, it is nice to see you *and* to be home, how are you doing?" she asked.

We had so much catching up to do, we could have benefited from a lady's night out.

"Come on in," I offered.

Ms. Joyce Ann stepped in, sat in her usual spot, the recliner by the window. She had no problem making herself at home. I didn't mind at all. She didn't visit often, when she did, she was welcomed with open arms.

"How was your trip?" I asked.

"Chile it was okay. I won about five thousand dollars," she shared like it was no big deal. "The show was a success. I sold most of my clothes," she added.

Ms. Joyce Ann took second place. Last year in New York, she placed first. She always departed full-handed and returned empty-handed, the opposite for most people who'd go on vacation. No more than five minutes passed, I was all caught up on the details of the fashion show. Next, she began to explain the situation with Tré. She knew I knew something, so there was no reason to beat around the bush.

Ms. Joyce Ann, up to no good, leaned forward, pulled the curtain back, and took a quick glimpse out the window to see if Sophia was on the porch. We both died laughing! She was fully aware Sophia would want to hear the scoop as well. Sophia was not at her post, which was becoming more routine.

While in Atlanta, Ms. Joyce Ann stumbled upon another participant who went by the name "Lady." After several days of communicating, the two began to exchange bits and pieces of information. Now, Ms. Joyce Ann was trusting of others, but she was not necessarily one to share her personal business. Apparently, she got caught up in being a little chatty. Perhaps she figured she was far enough from home and more than likely she would never see Lady again.

Comfortable in her new friendship, Ms. Joyce Ann chatted about how her ex-husband left her for a younger woman. Lady shared she had dated an older man. Nothing registered.

Who would have expected anything to register at that point...so many miles apart?

Shortly afterwards, Ms. Joyce Ann happened to mention Jerry's name. Verbalizing disbelief, Lady revealed that her ex's name was also Jerry. It was then the light bulb clicked!

"Jerry Johnson?" Lady questioned with hesitance.

"Yes Jerry Johnson," Ms. Joyce Ann answered.

Who would have ever thought that in a million years?

Lady declared she didn't know Jerry was married at the beginning of their dating; it wasn't until she fell in love with him that he told her he was getting a divorce. Ms. Joyce Ann found that funny; she never knew *he* had considered a divorce. She filed for divorce after he up and left. Jerry never responded in the allotted timeframe; therefore, the divorce was granted.

For some reason, I had a flashback of Isaac's dream confession, the affair was real even though it didn't seem possible. Ms. Joyce Ann went on to say Lady had come down one summer to visit her family. She met Jerry at a flea market one weekend. They talked, exchanged numbers, and everything advanced from there. When it came time for

Lady to return to Atlanta, Jerry said he would follow. She didn't believe he would, but he did.

Feeling the need to apologize, Lady expressed if she had to do things all over, the outcome would have been different. She pleaded for forgiveness. Ms. Joyce Ann assured her she wasn't at fault. She couldn't get mad at Jerry because she was so over it all. It had been years. Lady became pregnant and had Tré. She never married Jerry. Around the time Tré reached twelve years old, Jerry left her for another woman.

Ain't that some shit on top of some shit!

It was at that moment the two laughed so hard they couldn't stop.

Tré never saw Jerry again. Lady claimed she heard Jerry was living in a nursing home located about thirty minutes away from her residence. She never bothered to visit nor took the time to find out the details.

On to the part I couldn't comprehend...

Lady explained how Tré was such a good kid who needed a change in his life. He was twenty-five years old. He had anger issues. He wasn't receptive of his parents' age difference, felt embarrassed around his so-called friends, and he resented his father. Ms. Joyce Ann saddened by the story, was lured into meeting Tré. Supposedly they clicked. She said she could see him as her grandson. She saw the good in Tré, and agreed he needed a new start.

Ms. Joyce Ann offered for Tré to relocate and live with her for a while. *Weird!* Trusting the situation, she took it a step further and informed Lady she'd purchase him a plane ticket, he could fly in, and she'd have a key made for him. Tré was receptive. Lady was receptive because Tré was receptive. So that explained why the van had been in the driveway for a couple weeks. I was not sure why, out of all vehicles in the world, Tré ended up with a van rental. I didn't ask. My mind was already trying to absorb more details than my brain could withstand.

For the first time, I was not on the same page as Ms. Joyce Ann. I felt let down. *Had she lost her mind?* I would have never let a stranger come to my home, especially before me. Tré may have looked like a teenager, but I repeat, he was twenty-five freakin' years old! *Why was his ass still living with his mother in the first place?* Ms. Joyce Ann always trusted people, even though she got burned by Jerry. I never pried in people's business, nor did I put in my two cents unless asked, so I just listened, kept the straightest face possible, and prayed it would all work out.

Finally, Ms. Joyce Ann was able to locate Jerry. She visited to inform him she'd forgiven him. No foul intentions. She did not visit to showcase how she still had it going on and how successful she had been, but she genuinely visited to forgive him. Aware of his cancer, according to Tré, she didn't bother to throw it up in his face.

I struggled with my situation; I was not on Ms. Joyce Ann's level. She motivated me and was part of the reason why I didn't commit murder. I just couldn't see myself in her situation doing what she did. First, I would have slapped Lady as soon as I realized she was the woman my man left me for. Second, I would have told Jerry he was reaping what he sowed and to rot in hell. Third, I am not sure how I would have spoken to Tré, but I knew for sure he would not have been approved to come to my house.

Twenty-five? Hell to the no!

Ms. Joyce Ann was one of a kind! I loved her to the moon and back, but she lost brownie points on that one.

After listening to the drama, I was speechless. I was in shock. The Tré part stuck to me more than anything. All I could say was, "Wow!"

I told Ms. Joyce Ann she was indeed a special someone and Tré was blessed to have met her. I wished her well. Then, I informed her we needed to schedule a lunch date so I could fill her in on my love life. On that note, she stood up and prepared to leave. She peeped to see if Sophia was out. She was. She said she was going to go on over to Sophia's to catch her up…to get it over with. We both chuckled. Sophia would get a shorter version of the story.

Boy, if I was ever happy to see Sophia out on the porch in fluorescent colors, that was indeed the best time! Ms. Joyce Ann could go share her *own* story. I knew one thing for sure, if she had not been out, she had at least seen her come over. I didn't want to pretend like she hadn't told me anything if she asked. I was not one to lie, but I think I would have told a big fat one or two if that was the case. *What a story!*

Home Sweet Home

Vows are only as good as the person reciting them. When I married Isaac, I never imagined starting over. I had unconditional love for my Boo Bear. There was no other man on the face of the earth for me. He was *my* prince charming and the happy ending to my fairy tale. I loved Isaac with *all* four chambers of my heart. Agape love. We were inseparable.

"For better or worse" sounded great at the time I recited those words, when in reality, I only meant the first half, "for better." Of course, I knew there would be good times and bad times; my assumptions of bad times did not include *even if he cheated*. I had limits. When he cheated, his ass had to go!

Isaac and I never divorced. Even though *we* did not fully live up to our vows, they were never void. Through it all, I looked forward to my Boo Bear returning. He'd be on his last strike though. There were no three strikes and you're out rules here. More like two. Having a new addition to the family after I got my tubes tied, defeated the purpose. That meant someone else had some of *my* chocolate affection and was able to produce something I no longer could. Our family should have been closed to the public.

The kids were excited. They tidied their rooms without being instructed. Isaac Jr. taped about ten pieces of notebook paper together and created a colorful sign that read, "Welcome Back Dad, We Miss You!" JaRon added, "Home Sweet Home." Danielle wrote her little signature on it. Our kids were such compassionate kids. I could only hope Shantel wouldn't be the one bad apple to spoil the bunch. According to what I had heard, there's always one headache child. *How will she be when she grows up?*

"Mom here comes Dad!" Danielle shouted full of joy.

Yep, there was his truck. Benjamin was driving the truck while Isaac followed in the BMW. I must have been out of it back when he moved. I had no clue how his truck got to his apartment; never crossed my mind. He didn't know Benjamin then. Did Quintella drive it?

"Lord I have been doing well. Please do not let my questioning mind cause me to go crazy again. What happened has happened and I forgive Isaac," I said an emergency prayer.

It was nice to see Isaac had a work buddy. He and Benjamin seemed like they worked well together. I always feared Isaac would get out somewhere and pass out from heat exhaustion or hurt himself some way. To know someone accompanied him was reassuring.

144

Grinning ear to ear, Isaac and I jogged towards each other. We hugged so tightly, one of us could have ended up with a broken rib. Sophia was sitting out enjoying the view. All she needed was a bag of Orville Redenbacher popcorn and some seasoning salt.

"Hey Benjamin," I called out.

"Good afternoon Mrs. Singleton," he replied.

Isaac had his one sofa chair on the back of the truck and his bed and mattress. I'd worry about where we'd put them later. Danielle had gone to grab the boys. They leaped off the porch, causing the screen door to swing out to its max. They surrounded Isaac. I teared up. My family had reunited, approximately three hundred and sixty-five days later.

"Come on in Benjamin," I offered.

Benjamin hopped out the truck and entered the house for the first time.

"Make yourself comfortable." I said, expressing my hospitality.

Benjamin sat in Ms. Joyce Ann's favorite recliner. What she didn't know wouldn't hurt her. We hardly had company, so I had to coach the kids to speak. They greeted Benjamin respectfully.

"H-o-m-e sweet h-o-m-e," Isaac sang as he noticed the welcoming masterpiece from the kids. He hugged them all again while thanking them for the beautiful sign. I never heard my Boo Bear sing. He would have won an audition singing just those *three* words in his baritone voice. Barry White didn't have anything on my Isaac Pooh. He was elated to be home. It was the happiest I had ever seen him. I teared up again; the kind of tears I was used to. Tears of joy!

Isaac made his way out of the living room, leaving me alone with Benjamin.

"So, how is the wife and baby coming along?" I questioned.

"Oh, I am not married, but things are going well. She has about three more months to go," he explained.

All I could think about was Quintella getting pregnant by a married man. I wondered if he had someone else's wife pregnant, or if he was just dating around. Also, I wondered if he had been searching for a new job, or if he relied on Isaac for full-time employment. Though tempted to pry, I managed to stay in my lane. It was his business. Isaac never shared information unless I asked. I gathered men failed to realize withholding information was deemed a marital crime. Women viewed it as being secretive. If it were meant for me to find out, I had no doubt I'd find out in due time.

I offered Benjamin a glass of water. He said he was good. I turned on the TV and offered him the remote. He said he was good. Hell, I didn't know what else to do or talk about. I was extremely glad to see Isaac strut back into the living room; feeling odd in my own home was not cutting it for me.

"Well suga, I am going to run Benjamin home," he announced.

"Okay," I replied.

"Thank you for helping Isaac. I am sure you have been a life saver. Lord knows I used to worry about my baby out there in the heat all alone." I expressed my appreciation and wifely concerns.

"No, *thank you*! I appreciate Isaac allowing me the opportunity to make a little money until I can get back on my feet. It has been mighty helpful. A blessing." Benjamin expressed his return appreciation.

Isaac had Benjamin help to lift the furniture out of the truck and carry it to the garage. Isaac never parked his truck in the third spot, so there was plenty of room. At least it was not like they were putting junk in the garage. I've seen some junky garages in my lifetime; I doubt I could tolerate a bunch of garbage. My man was just a neat freak all round kinda guy; so many reasons to love him.

"Thank You, Lord," I praised my Savior.

Isaac was home sweet home. I called for Isaac Jr. to close the door. Sophia was still on alert, and as usual I wasn't ready for what she had in store.

Unaware of the family plan for the remainder of the day, I figured I'd prepare the very first meal I ever cooked for Isaac: catfish, buttered corn on the cob, homemade fries, and a chef salad. I didn't want history to repeat itself. However, I did want him to realize what he had been missing. I may have been clueless of what other wives did for *their* spouses, but I knew I cooked for *my* man every day, and I made sure he had lunch to carry out for work. I knew I was a wife who stayed up late to give *my* man what I called *sleep medicine*. If Isaac didn't realize what he truly had while he was gone, then I'd say he was both the stupidest *and* the sexiest man alive.

I had Danielle help to set the table. Isaac Jr. helped peel the potatoes for the fries, and JaRon rinsed off the lettuce for the salad. I informed the kids we would wait until Dad got back to decide if we'd watch a movie or play a family game.

"I am so glad Dad is back home," Danielle said in her sweet little girl voice.

"Yeah me too," both Isaac Jr. and JaRon said simultaneously.

"Well good. I am happy to have him back as well. By the way, your little sister will be staying over every Wednesday and every other Saturday,"

I felt it was a good time to add enlightenment.

"Yay! Will she sleep in my room?" Danielle asked.

"Let's see what your dad has to say." I answered.

Everyone was happy. You would have thought it was Christmas in the Singleton house.

Shantel is in the House

"Isaac, get her!" I yelled as Shantel crawled towards the wall outlet.

"No Pumpkin!" Isaac shouted as he made two long struts to reach her.

Pumpkin?

"Why Pumpkin?" I asked not believing the nickname I was hearing.

"Oh baby, I guess that hadn't registered to me. I've said Pumpkin but yes, I will work on another name. Sorry." Isaac responded, realizing I wasn't having it.

Rev. Dickerson called Quintella his Pumpkin. There was not going to be any Quintellas or Pumpkins in our house. Yes, he had to come up with another nickname for sure.

How could that have not registered?

Shantel was now six months. She was crawling and getting into everything. I was freakin' out, worried something could happen to her while she was over our house. True, Isaac kept her on his days, obviously he had done a great job. However, I just felt on edge all the time, like I had to watch her constantly. While everyone else was going about worry free, I was stressing and beginning to question if I was ready to be a stepmother to a child at such level. Even though I had chosen to move forward with Isaac, having a child under five was like a setback for a mother who had already mothered past those stages.

"Get her, damnit!" I hollered, not meaning to curse.

Shantel had a strong grip on the curtain and was pulling at it.

"All I need is for her to yank the darn thang down and the rod hit her in the head, ugh…," I expressed a potential result.

Isaac Jr. raced to swoop her up before the reality could exist.

"Evette, how about you go take a break. Everything is going to be okay. I got this," Isaac suggested.

I was told to "go take a break," like I was the problem. Keeping Shantel was not going to be as pleasant as I thought. She was too busy for my nerves. If something happened to her, I would have had to deal with false accusations. Trust me, nobody would have wanted to go there with me.

Finally, after scavenging all throughout the living room, the little daredevil wore herself out and fell asleep. Isaac placed her in the crib he purchased just before he brought her over. We decided to keep her in our room the first few visits. She'd go into Danielle's room soon to follow.

JaRon was into his portable Nintendo DS, while Danielle was playing with her Barbie doll styling head. I honestly thought she'd be more attentive to her little sister. After about fifteen minutes of patty cake, Danielle went on about her business as though Shantel was not around. Isaac Jr. was gazing at the end of The Wizard of Oz on the flat screen. Seemed like the kids pick that movie at least once a month. I don't know what it was about it.

Evidently, the kids realized it was different seeing their half-sister for a few hours here and there, compared to having her in the house long term, robbing them of their attention.

"Okay, kids, time for bed. You have school tomorrow," I continued with the routine house rules while Isaac was in the process of drifting off on the sofa.

Shantel slept until about five o'clock in the morning. I thought at six months, babies slept at least until seven or eight o'clock. Oh no, not *Pumpkin*.

Isaac did get up to pamper her needs, but it was not like I could just drift back off to sleep. The kids had to get up at 7:30. School started by 8:45. If I allowed myself to go back to sleep, I'd have to get back up anyway. I guess Isaac and I didn't talk the *during the week* thing through. We were so happy of the possibility of being a family again, we didn't really plan all the details of the return.

Isaac woke the kids up and took them to school. He took Shantel along for the ride. He advised me to rest a few more hours. I must confess, I felt a tad guilty; I figured he must have picked up on my demeanor, but I was cool with that. I kept my butt right in bed and slept like I was *the* baby. I slept until about ten o'clock.

When I went out to the kitchen, Isaac had my breakfast on the table for once. He had made some blueberry pancakes, bacon, and scrambled eggs. He had Shantel in a Winnie the Pooh bouncer. He must have had it in the trunk of his car. I didn't eyeball it at his place. Perhaps, he purchased it when he bought the crib.

"You mean to tell me you knew how to cook all these years?" I asked, trying to have a sense of humor.

"You bet," Isaac replied, leaning forward to kiss me on the cheek.

I realized I needed to start back praying. Since everything had been all honky dory, I hadn't prayed as much. Isaac taking the kids to school showed me he knew having Shantel over would be a lot. It showed he would step up to the plate and at least try to make my days easier.

"Thank You, Lord. Please continue to work with me. I need more patience. Please remove any resentful feelings from my heart. Amen," I prayed.

The food was outstanding. I didn't leave one crumb on my plate. I complimented Isaac on his chef skills. He stood there proud, in his white chef apron the kids bought him for Father's Day several years ago. Honestly, it was the first time he'd ever worn it.

"Well…what time will baby girl need to be home?" I asked.

"Usually, I have her home by three o'clock. Quintella is giving me until four o'clock on Wednesdays. She knows I may have to pick up the kids from school," Isaac provided more specifics than his usual.

"I guess the two of you get along pretty well, huh?" I asked.

"I imagine so." That time he replied with not as much feedback as I preferred.

I spoke too soon.

Isaac's and Quintella's relationship was a little bit too on the friendly side for me. They got along. No disputes. *Did she have him wrapped around her fingers? Was she using the baby to eventually snag my man?*

The mental struggle was real. I figured the next time I saw Dr. Gregg; I would update her on my love life and convince her I still needed my prescription for Xanax. She never allowed refills without a follow up office visit. I guess I had to prove I was still a Xanax candidate or something. Even if I had advanced past the need, I was smart enough to put on an act to get what I wanted. The upcoming weekend was

Isaac's weekend to keep Shantel too… That was only two days away. Yep, a refill was urgent alright. At least his weekends were Saturday through Sunday and not Friday through Sunday. I recognized the following Wednesday would be easier. Afterwards, I'd have seven days of normalcy.

Isaac gathered up Shantel and her belongings, leaving the bouncer behind. He planned to pick up the kids from school and take Shantel home. I gave her a little kiss on the cheek as she was probably babbling to tell me how she really felt. I kissed Isaac on the lips; they headed out. For some reason I felt a sense of relief when I saw his car pull away. It was like a load had been lifted.

Would it be like this every time?

After reflecting on the day and a half, I was pleased with my efforts. I helped as much as my energy allowed. I changed Shantel's diaper a few times and I fed her right after she arrived. The kids only played with her off and on. Maybe they were feeling some kind of way. Everything was new to everyone. I could only wait to see what the weekend would bring. Until then, I prayed and made my follow-up appointment to see Dr. Gregg.

Sophia's Puzzle Pieces

After much needed rest, I felt refreshed. Isaac had already departed into the fields. I didn't get out of bed to cook his breakfast, or to prepare his black, no cream or sugar added coffee. No lunch. Boy, talking about a change! It was not on purpose; I must have slept through my alarm, or Isaac must have turned it off when he came to bed. No sex! Jesus, what was going on? I swung out of bed, hurried to the kids' rooms. They were off to school. Isaac left a note on the door to Danielle's room, knowing I'd check her room first. He had talked to Ms. Joyce Ann; told her I was sleep and asked if she could take the kids to school. Wow, talking about scary! My kids had moved about throughout the house, prepared for school, and left without my awareness. Surely, Isaac had to instruct them not to awaken me. JaRon would have at least said bye for sure.

I showered up, put on my usual around the house and out to the mailbox clothes. Isaac had a little bowl of grits sitting on the table with some French toast. *The man had me cooking my ass off for nine years when all along he knew how to cook!* I was so caught up in my wifely duties; I was clueless on what skills my husband had, other than landscaping work and being Mr. Fixer Upper.

Don't get me wrong, I was loving it. Heck, I deserved it!

I headed to thank Ms. Joyce Ann; however, she was still out and about. The van was gone as well. Tré must have been running around. They didn't seem to have any issues living together. Ms. Joyce Ann's routine didn't seem affected. She was back to passing candies to the kids in the neighborhood. Hmm…maybe she needed a little house guest. People seem to always point out no matter how happy they are, something is always missing. He could have been the child she always wanted. His age evidently didn't matter. Who knows?

Since I was not able to thank Ms. Joyce Ann, I figured I'd hot tail it on across to Sophia's. There was no need to keep her in the dark forever. There were plenty of moments she could have come over to pry, but for the last couple weeks she had surprised me. Even though she was grown and all…perhaps she had grown past the prying in other people's business stage.

"Hey lady. How are you doing today? Hadn't talked to you in a minute," I said as I approached.

"Blessed and highly favored. Yeah, I see you've been avoiding me," Sophia commented.

Welp, she nailed it! I rambled on how I had been so busy and had so much going on, hoping to justify my avoidance.

"Yeah, I see you over there chile…just running like a little busy bee," Sophia validated my justification.

No doubt she did see me. There were a few days the curtains were open.

"I see you know ole boy Benjamin," Sophia said unexpectedly.

"Yes, we met him at our new church, Sky's the Limit Baptist Church. Isaac agreed to give him a little work until he can get back on his feet. How do you know him?" I asked.

Why did I ask?

Sophia had a handful to deliver! Or should I say a mouth full. She knew Benjamin Michael from the mini mart. She claimed he used to work there but got fired for missing too many days. *He told Isaac he had gotten laid off. Lie number one was revealed.*

According to Sophia, Benjamin had gotten some chick pregnant. He claimed she had been using his car a lot and not getting it back to him in time so he could make it to work. The weird part was, Benjamin had some woman pregnant, but the woman was officially seeing another woman.

"So, he was just a sperm donor?" I questioned.

157

I couldn't help but pry. Sophia was putting out some good gossip.

"Chile, I don't know what he was. The entire story makes no sense to me. He has a baby on the way. She wants him to support the baby, but she wants to share the baby with her partner who also has a baby," she gossiped on.

"His ass saw me sitting over here when he came by y'all's house. I don't know why he didn't speak. I started to yell out his name. If I had a rock, I would have chunked it at his butt, as much as we be talking. He knew good and well he saw me," Sophia vented on and on longer than I anticipated.

She wasn't lying about the seeing her part...you can't miss her!

"I figure I'd give him a piece of my mind next time I see him!" Sophia emphasized, now angered.

"Well people are something else, so I know what you mean," I replied.

That was the first time I witnessed frustration in Sophia. A nerve had been hit. I thought I was one bad mama jama; hell, the sista put fear in another sista with the tone in her voice. To reduce my heartrate, I decided I'd update her on *my* status. She'd ask eventually, so I head-started her to the continuation of my life story. The last time I visited, I told her Isaac was returning. She had seen he was back, so I picked up where I left off.

Sophia was all caught up on our business now. She had calmed down. Being that I was drawn into the prying business during our conversation, I figured I'd take advantage to use the time to ask who on earth did she talk to on the phone all the time. Come to find out she was not talking to anyone. Instead, she was listening to Pandora. She would hold the phone up to her ear majority of the time because she kept the volume low. Rather than talking, she was singing the words to the songs. That explained why she would be waving the phone in the air from time to time and swaying back and forth. Sophia was over there getting her groove on.

Other times she was listening to YouTube videos on how to make certain foods. When I assumed she was just over there jabbering away, she was reciting the ingredients. Having one hand was too much of a hassle to write down the recipes. By repeating them over and over, she could recall what items to get when she made her journey to the mini mart. Every week she tried a new recipe. She'd listen to the same video at least three to five times to memorize not only the ingredients, but also to learn how to prepare each meal.

Sophia had plenty of cookbooks. She said listening to recipes and being able to recall them was more meaningful to her. It was like exercise to her brain. I was so outdone; I didn't know what to think. There I was, along with Ms. Joyce Ann from time to time, thinking the woman was crazy as all get out and just gossiping her days away. All along, she was doing something halfway constructive. For the first time I couldn't wait to see Ms. Joyce Ann so I could enlighten her on what I had just learned. One of the most common phrases I'd heard was "Assuming makes an ass out of you." Ain't that the truth.

After speaking with Sophia, I had new respect for her. Yes, she could be a pain in the butt from time to time, and she was nosey as hell, but the lady was not just sitting on her porch every day gossiping. We thought so for nine years! It made me wonder how well people really know their neighbors.

I updated Sophia on Isaac and me. Surprisingly, she didn't have any questions. No sarcastic comments. As a matter of fact, she reminded me that Isaac was *my* boo. She told me not to let any woman interfere with my marriage, which was a repeat of what she had told me once before. She may have been an instigator, but she cared about my marriage more than I thought. Sophia won my heart that day. I viewed her differently from that day on. My respect for her was equal to the respect I had for Ms. Joyce Ann. Her two cents finally mattered!

My revelation led me to think about Gina, how I saw her just about every day, but we never had a long conversation; partly because I never gave her an opportunity to say more than two to three sentences. I wasn't trying to make new friends. I concluded it was time to start building my friend list. Talking about a reality check. I literally had been a mess for years. The need to repent was eating at my heart. I decided the upcoming Sunday would be my repent day.

"God, thank You for today. I have learned so much. Amen." I released my faults to God.

160

Ms. Joyce Ann's Puzzle Pieces

Cheerful to miserable, ecstatic to furious, life had been one ginormous rollercoaster ride, full of valleys and mountains, twists and turns, and coincidental circumstances. Struggles were real. Willie Mae seemingly embedded my mind with plenty of scriptures, quotes, or what she'd call "facts of life."

She shared, "God *never* puts more on you than you can bear."

Well…I didn't know what my bear maximum was, but I knew there were times I believed I had reached it.

Another perspective, in truth, Willie Mae's quote or fact of life was a reality check. If God never put more on me than I could bear, that must have meant He created me to be one strong sista. Thinking so highly of me was a compliment. I know, weird. Perhaps He knew another sista would have gone off the deep end by now. I've had insane moments, but at the same time I was strong enough not to fall off the cliff. God had faith in me.

History reveals my temperamental issues. My nerves dwelled in standby mode, easily activated. Xanax was the quick fix. Prayer helped. I pridefully patted myself on the back on more than one occasion; I never did anything drastic that could have possibly landed me behind bars. Several times I was saved by the bell. Nobody but God. Now on the other hand, if my thoughts alone could have convicted me, I'd be serving a life sentence.

While conversing with Sophia, I encountered a rude awakening. Not only did I learn an abundance about Sophia, but also, I learned an abundance about myself.

Ready to share my experience to Ms. Joyce Ann, I rushed over as soon as I returned from dropping the kids off at school. This time you could say I was the Sophia, the messenger delivering news to someone else. Ms. Joyce Ann and I had misjudged Sophia. I was not pleased; however, I was excited to share my new discovery.

It was hard to tell when Tré was home because the van had been returned to the rental company. Ms. Joyce Ann may have been a little looney for allowing him to stay, but she knew better than to allow him to drive her car. *She had some sense left in that nugget.* Sometimes he'd walk places. Other times, I noticed a car would come by to pick him up. To my understanding, Lady still had family up this way. He could have been with family. I never asked.

The door was open. I could see Ms. Joyce Ann knitting clothes. I tapped on the screen. I was given the okay to enter. She was knitting clothes for Gina's children; not because they needed any, but because that was what she did. Everyone on the block had a little Ms. Joyce Ann, but in a good way. She had met Gina since she returned from Atlanta; providing clothes was just her way of welcoming newbies to the neighborhood.

Gina ended up not being a bother or threat at all. She exercised every day; that's about it. She stayed to herself from what I could tell. I was cool with that. I figured the next time I saw her; I'd make a greater effort to initiate conversation. I even thought I'd see if she'd be interested in having an exercise buddy. I needed a motivator to be successful. I loved being alone, but I just couldn't see myself working up a sweat all by myself…at least not while exercising.

"I thought I'd stop by to finally catch you up on the Singleton house. And then I can't wait to tell you about my latest discovery." I attempted to build suspense.

"I've been waiting to hear from you girl, but you know how we are…in due time," Ms. Joyce Ann replied.

Refusing to waste another minute, I shared everything regarding Isaac and me, starting from the day she left for Atlanta. I included all my church experiences, how we met Benjamin, my run in with my old classmate, the phone call from Isaac's baby's mama…I shared it all.

Ms. Joyce Ann continued with her knitting. It was like my life story gave her a little rhythm; she was just a goin'. Pleased to know Isaac and I were working things out, she commended me on my decision to let Isaac return home. Without asking for her input, she mentioned that Isaac should have never moved out in the first place.

Ms. Joyce Ann prophesied how she knew he'd be back. She then went on to say that our problems were not over. That was scary!

What did she mean they were not over? What did she know that I didn't know?

All I could think was, "It better be over!"

Putting my love-hate life to the side, I provided Ms. Joyce Ann with a little enlightenment on Sophia and her *phone calling*. I included the information Sophia relayed about Benjamin. As I shared the information, she kept saying, "I see." She said it so often eventually I paused my storytelling to inquire about what it was that she was "seeing." Those were just not routine words to depart from her mouth; I knew something was up.

"Evette, I think you're missing out on something," Ms. Joyce Ann expressed while she refrained from knitting.

She was just as shocked as I was about Sophia's routine. We both learned and felt guilty for our misconceptions. We agreed one day we would have to confess to Sophia, but also agreed the one day would be much later down the line.

164

"Now, I am about to tell you something sweetheart. From what I can gather you didn't pick it up from your encounter with Sophia. I believe she may have revealed something that even she was unaware of, involving you more than Benjamin my dear," Ms. Joyce Ann continued.

What now?

"I've sat here and listened to everything you told me and immediately I am able to visualize it all," Ms. Joyce Ann said, elevating my fear of the unknown.

"What's going on? If you know something, please share it with me!" I begged for the first time in my life.

Ms. Joyce Ann explained how she concluded Benjamin was the one who had Michelle Lee pregnant. That was why she never said she was married when I saw her. She mentioned Michelle Lee must have been in a relationship with Quintella. That was why Michelle Lee claimed having a stepdaughter. She pointed out that when I saw Michelle Lee in the grocery store, she already knew I was still with Isaac. She was just messing with me to see what my response would be. She added Quintella called me the following day acting like she was looking for Isaac. That was just part of their game. That explained why Quintella said she had been "notified."

The worst part of it all…She said Isaac must have known everything because he was close to Benjamin and had to know his situation.

Between Sophia and Ms. Joyce Ann, Sophia laid out the puzzle pieces and Ms. Joyce Ann started putting the darn pieces together. There I was gazing at an almost completed puzzle! It was then I saw everything! She was 100% correct.

"Well I be damned again!" I cried out. "You're right! You're absolutely correct! I recall driving down Camille Street one day. I made a few turns. I saw Isaac and Benjamin working on a yard together. There were baby toys outside. It was not one of Isaac's routine houses. I bet that was Michelle Lee's house. Quintella had to have moved in. She used to stay in a studio house behind her dad's house."

I was adding the final puzzle pieces. "Benjamin immediately said he was not married when I asked him how his marriage was," I rambled on. "Oh my God, if I ain't the damn fool for the umpteenth time!" I cried on and on.

Ms. Joyce Ann pushed aside her knitting table and stood up. She tiptoed over to embrace me like I was a baby. I gave in. All pride aside, I wept like a baby who had a bottle right before his or her eyes but couldn't reach out to get it. I was at my wit's end! Embarrassed, pissed, cheated, just altogether outdone! Though I had snot pouring everywhere, Ms. Joyce Ann pampered me like I was her own. I was numb. I couldn't do anything for myself. She held and loved on me for at least fifteen minutes.

Ms. Joyce Ann, with her soothing voice, continued to console me, while attempting to at least convince me Isaac had not cheated me, but instead he had failed to keep me in the loop. She pleaded for me to at least understand that. She tried to cover for him by saying he was torn between two households. He was trying to keep peace and be a man on both sides. She assured me I was his primary love. She advised me to talk to him later without screaming and yelling. Immediately she admitted this must have been the *more to come* she envisioned. She just didn't know it would be so sudden.

Boy, I knew love could cause one to be blinded of a few things. I didn't see any of this when everything was right before my eyes. That darn Michelle Lee was probably laughing in my face. Quintella was stirring up trouble being revengeful, as though I had wronged her. While I was calling everyone else out of their names and making assumptions about their lives, I was oblivious to what was happening in my own. All I knew when I left Ms. Joyce Ann's was, I was tired of being the darn fool! I loved Isaac, but I was fed up. I felt the ding-dong had left me hanging one time too many…good intentions or not!

Pity Party

Just when I thought I was ready to repent, I had to put that thought on hold. I had a new respect for Sophia, and a new heart for Gina, but I was not ready to be born again. There was no use of me playing with the Lord's Holy Water. I could only pray I'd be all squared away before the rapture. As Forrest Gump said, "Life is like a box of chocolates. You never know what you're gonna get."

I would have been all the rejected chocolates. If my life were a box of fireworks, I'd be all the duds. I was Mrs. Humpty Dumpty, or at least some kin. One thing for sure, I had some great falls.

Why me?

I swear I'd made significant attitude improvements. I had learned a lot. I was willing to open more to society. I literally let go and cried to Ms. Joyce Ann, something I would have never done. I shared some of my life stories with her throughout the years. She had seen me upset over and over before, but she had never seen me boo hoo and snot all over the place; really, neither had I.

My husband cheated on me and made a baby by another woman. Yet, I took him back and accepted a baby that wasn't mine. *What else did I need to do? What else would I have to go through? Why was I always left out of the loop?*

I'd been a faithful wife. I was involved in my kids' lives, an excellent mother. I attended church, and at one point I worked a part-time job. I didn't drink hard liquor, didn't smoke, didn't do drugs…I was confused. I knew people who did all the above, and they seemed to live an upbeat life. Surely, I was done reaping what I had sown in high school. *What in the heck was going on?* Every time I thought I saw the light at the end of the tunnel, darkness invaded my destination. It reminded me of the glass-mirrored mazes at the state fair. How many times would I have to bump into things before I would be freed?

Xanax stopped doing the trick. Dr. Gregg prescribed me some Lexapro, an antidepressant. Maybe she saw it coming. Lord knows I didn't. I filled the prescription for the record, but never took it. After my puzzle solving experience, another solution was for me to start taking my Lexapro. I recalled it would take weeks to take effect. If I had known everything was going to fall apart, I surely would have started it when advised. No more *Mama knows best*. More like doctor knows best.

There I was approaching my thirties and taking crazy medications. Ms. Joyce Ann was in her eighties, only taking vitamins and she'd been through a few valleys herself. She was happy. Gina appeared happy. Sophia was content. Quintella and Michelle Lee were living the best of both worlds. Meanwhile, there I was all down and out like a drug addict who had hit rock bottom. They say, "What goes up must come down." All I could pray for then was what goes down, must go up.

"Lord lift me! I am really trying! I have learned my lesson! Please renew me! I need a new start! Order my steps dear Lord! Amen," I begged and prayed.

After examining my life, I accepted I had made many efforts to live pleasing in God's sight, but I did conclude I never gave my 100%. I was ready to give 100%. There was no way my life could get worse than what it had been. I surrendered all. It was like Willie Mae dwelled inside of me. I was constantly camouflaging her spirit with my evil one. The battle was on. Well, she won! I decided the battle was no longer mine, it was the Lord's!

I still had intentions to talk with Isaac. I just preferred to wait until after Shantel's weekend had passed. It was going on her third weekend to sleep over. Things had gotten a little less stressful with each visit. The kids had come along a little better and were spending more time with their half-sister. Danielle was happy to share her room. Shantel finally slept through the nights, so Danielle's sleep was not interrupted.

In the meantime, I did something I had not done in years, I pulled out my New Living Translation Bible and began reading the first chapter of the Gospel of Matthew; the New Testament. I read all the way to the end of John. It was time for me to do some more soul searching. Willie Mae swore the day would come for me to bow down and let go and let God. As far as I was concerned, He could have it!

Communication: The Key

Church was awesome as usual. The worship and sermon could not have been any better. The kids enjoyed their third visit to children's church. It was not Shantel's weekend that go round, so it was just *the originals*.

Isaac and Benjamin had their usual after church chat in the parking lot. Everything was going smoothly. From church, we ventured on over to Bob's Buffet for the kids' sake.

I was ready to confront Isaac about my findings, but I promised myself I'd wait until we returned home and settled for bed. I wasn't as frustrated anymore; however, I still deserved an explanation from him. I wanted to know why he didn't feel the need to share certain information with me. Being the last one to know something was an insult. I was not cool with that. I was tired of feeling like the laughingstock on the block. I had an uneasy feeling every time I went somewhere. I wondered if people knew something about me...I was already considered light weight crazy. Well...the situation was not helping.

After the buffet, Isaac surprised the kids with a visit to the park. He surprised me as well. I guess you could say it was another occasion where I found out after the fact. Squirrel's Park was about five miles from the house. The park was known for its name. I used to believe the park was not designed for humans. Over time, it became the hangout spot for nearby families. The kids would go just to play tag football and things of that nature. The girls stood around and cheered on the boys like there was an actual youth game going on. There was a tetherball pole there. Now, that used to be *my* game back in the day. It didn't take much to entertain the kids; one thing I enjoyed about not having teenagers. I heard they could be a mess! There was a pool that had been shut down for the season. Not much to the park, but the kids seemed to enjoy the place.

While the kids ran around getting their exercise, Isaac and I sat on a nearby bench and looked on. I decided the mood was right to initiate my concerns. Why wait when the opportunity was fitting? I figured I'd get it out of the way. Therefore, by night I could rest up and get some good sleep. I had tossed and turned the prior night, juggling the puzzle pieces in my mind...able to connect more and more things together.

"Isaac, over the last few days, there have been situations revealed to me that have really hurt my feelings," I began in a calm and caring voice.

"What's been on your mind Evette?" Isaac asked with concern in his voice.

I took the opportunity and ran with it. I expressed how I felt cheated. Not knowing he was keeping up with Quintella's house, as well as ours irked me. I explained how he must have known when I mentioned seeing Michelle Lee in the store, that she and Quintella were a couple. Continuing to vent, I made known I didn't appreciate him working with Benjamin, knowing all along he had a baby on the way by Michelle Lee.

Just as Ms. Joyce Ann forewarned me, Isaac admitted he knew all. He just wanted to keep peace. In his narrowed thinking, he didn't see anything wrong with cutting Quintella's and Michelle Lee's grass and keeping their lawn up. He and Benjamin came to a mutual agreement it was the least they could do, being that Quintella was the mother of his kid and Michelle Lee was an expectant mother of Benjamin's.

I wanted to but in and say, women could cut yards just like men, but I tell you, God was working with me. When Isaac first met Benjamin, he didn't realize Michelle Lee was the expectant mom until he cut the yard for the first time. That was all to that part of the story.

Isaac attempted to justify his reason for not telling me. He claimed he didn't see it as a big deal. I was the love of his life and the one he returned home to every night. Even though I was the love of his life, and the one he returned home to every night, I continued to keep my extra comments to myself, as much as I wanted to say it didn't matter before.

He reminded me of my temper. Apparently, he was protecting me. He was being preventative! *Afterall, a husband's duty is to protect his wife, right?*

Evidently, Benjamin met Michelle Lee at the mini mart. He knew Quintella and Michelle Lee resided together. He didn't find out they were a couple until after the fact. According to Isaac, Benjamin felt he was tricked into being a father. *Sound familiar?* So, as I presumed, he was just the sperm donor. Poor Benjamin spent several nights with Michelle Lee while Quintella was out of town seeing her mother. He was booted out once she returned. He was basically homeless. After working with Isaac, he was able to lease an apartment just a few apartments down from Isaac's.

Benjamin reminded me of myself. I was a hard-working and faithful sista. He sounded like a hard-working brother who was trying to live pleasing in God's sight. Despite being homeless at the time, he made his way to church every Sunday and was an active member on the Greeter's committee. He had transportation. Unfortunately, his transportation had been his home.

176

Isaac was tricked by Rev. Dickerson and Quintella, who had finally moved from underneath her father's wings. Benjamin was tricked by Michelle Lee. Life was unpredictable! It was a small world! Out of all the churches I could have chosen, I chose one where a man attended who would become friends with my husband, just for him to have a baby by a lady whose partner already had a baby by my husband. Did you follow that?

Michelle Lee had the honor of being Shantel's stepmother, while I also had the honor of being her stepmother! The two girls who disliked me in school were now tied to my life forever! Normally, the thought of something like this would have caused me to say a few choice words.

Progress!

I knew Isaac had to be impressed by my calm demeanor. Trust me, I was impressed as well. I had a sense of peace about it all. I desired to keep fighting for my marriage. Like Ms. Joyce Ann pointed out, it was not like Isaac laid down with another woman again. He just needed to know how detrimental it could be keeping information from his wife. Once again, I was willing to give *my* Boo Bear another shot, a clean slate.

I updated Isaac on my religious goals, how I wanted to live a life more pleasing to the Lord. I shared I was back to reading my Bible and how it would be a nightly routine before any love making. He was cool with that. We used to pray as a family. I believe our problems began when we stopped. Yeah, that is what it was!

Isaac Jr. was telling all the kids on the field the rules of the game according to how *he* saw them. It was funny to see the kids playing and running wildly around like they knew the game, adding and subtracting rules as they went. Danielle had met up with a few little girls. They were offbeat, cheering on the game. Such a precious sight to see. Isaac placed his arms around my neck. We just sat there and watched the kids enjoy their innocence. It was amazing to see a group of kids getting along, with no fussing and no fighting.

New Babysitter Assistant

Tré freeloaded off Ms. Joyce Ann for several months. He met a hoochie mama somewhere while out and about. Despite Ms. Joyce Ann's hospitality, he was unappreciative, and he was not pleased that his girlfriend was not privileged to join his free rent residence.

The nerve of him with his inconsiderate expectations!

For a girl to be okay moving in with someone she hadn't met, it revealed that her maturity was on the same level as Tré's, with his twenty-five-year-old self.

See, that right there made me want to slap my own kids and say, "I wish you would!"

One day while Ms. Joyce Ann was out and about, Tré moved out; the fool didn't even bother to say thank you…he just up and left. I'd say like father like son. I could vibe the runaway bothered Ms. Joyce Ann, but as with all other experiences, she said, "His loss."

She kept doing her thang; the Ms. Joyce Ann I knew. I was not sure if Lady was updated; I didn't ask. As a matter of fact, I never heard her name again.

After Tré left, Ms. Joyce Ann started up a knitting class from her house. Every Monday through Thursday she'd have friends over for classes. She taught them how to make scarves and hats to start, and then they advanced to shirts and dresses. Charging little or nothing for her services, Ms. Joyce Ann did make a little money out of it. Remind you, for being in her eighties, my neighbor sista was living the life. I was surprised to find out Gina took classes. It was not like she worked, so, why not? I am sure she had plenty of spare time. Since the classes were early in the morning, Ms. Joyce Ann wasn't available to help as much with the kids. I quit my job, but sometimes Isaac and I would come up with plans; she was the only one we confided in.

Benjamin was over more frequently with Isaac, not only cutting the grass, but also working on minor house updates and repairs. He seemed to be a trustworthy man from what I gathered. He grew on me. Eventually, the kids started speaking without being reminded, and Benjamin would try to hold little conversations with them. I didn't see anything wrong with allowing Benjamin to sit with the kids from time to time if needed. I presented my idea to Isaac. He trusted the situation. Benjamin happily accepted the offer. Though Ms. Joyce Ann kept the kids for free, we figured we'd pay a small amount for any assistance Benjamin provided.

Sophia finally called Benjamin out on ignoring her. Come to find out, he never noticed her on her porch. He didn't bother to look her direction. He apologized. She forgave him. Other than her mini-mart concerns with Benjamin, Sophia didn't have any other negatives to share. She said he was always polite at work. He flirted with her a few times, but never got too far out of his lane. Whether he was fired or laid off no longer mattered. The bottom line was he missed work due to Michelle Lee taking the car and not getting it back on time for him to report to work.

I never imagined a man babysitter, especially babysitting my daughter who was now seven years of age, in the second grade. JaRon was nine years old, in the fourth grade, and Isaac Jr., was eleven years old, and finally had made his way to middle school. I figured after another year; Jr. would be able to watch the younger two. Shantel was nearing the eleven-month mark. Isaac and I avoided making plans on her days; no one else could baby-sit her. Benjamin knew Quintella and all, but we didn't want him to babysit Shantel. Michelle Lee was about to pop any day; we figured he could keep his own baby when the time came. According to Benjamin, Michelle Lee at least promised he'd be able to father his baby if he wanted. *Who wouldn't? She was married to Quintella, but he was still the father! He had rights!*

Since Benjamin was expected to help Isaac later around the house, I decided to put on presentable clothes and to make my famous Italian spaghetti. I assumed he'd be hungry as well, so why not make a little extra for the man who was helping *my* man. Isaac told me once that

Benjamin's refrigerator rarely had food in it. He'd only see sandwich meat and bottles of water. His apartment was on the empty side. He had no furniture, just a mattress and a wooden chair. He owned a small TV and a square folding table, like the one my father used to play dominoes on with his friends when I was a child. Poor man. I couldn't build up enough nerves to ask Isaac if he could have his old apartment furniture. It would have at least freed up space in the garage.

I had empathy for Benjamin. I felt his pain. He was a good man striving to make it in the trying world. I was a living witness to what it was like to be a target; to have darts tossed at you over and over while shielding your own heart. Though I didn't know his entire life story; it had not been told, it didn't matter. He was good people, just needed a little help until he could get back on his feet. I was so proud of Isaac for opening his heart to allow someone to work for him. They became good friends; a win-win situation.

Using my handheld can opener, I eventually opened a couple cans of Green Giant French Style Green Beans. As I twisted the handle, the opening part was not smooth sailing. I ended up using a knife to help pry open the lid, taking extra precautions not to cut my finger. Been there, done that. I requested an electric opener several times over the years for Christmas. I must have been on Santa's naughty list because that request had never been granted. Anyway, I seasoned the beans to perfection and tossed together a little salad, a food choice for just about every Singleton meal. I made homemade rolls. Finally, I brewed up some good ole fashioned tea. Nothing like having a hot meal ready for a good man after a hard day's work. In that case...a hot meal for two good men.

Help to the Rescue

Nothing much was happening in the neighborhood. Sophia was not posted. Ms. Joyce Ann was out and about. Gina had already accomplished her lap around the circle. Kids were at school. Isaac and Benjamin were tending to lawns. Finally, a good day to check out Pebble's Wigs and Beauty Store. My hair hadn't fallen out anymore, but it sho hadn't filled in either. I needed a little something for me. I kept up with everyone else's beauty; I failed to keep up with my own. Funny, my life had been all about me, looking at it one way, when, in actuality, it had not been about me at all.

Pebble's Wig and Beauty Store was in the same parking lot as the mini mart. I hated the parking lot; it was better to park in the street, rather than taking the risk of getting flat tires. There was a dumpster between the two buildings; however, the trash seemed to make it everywhere other than its destination. I never understood where the rocks came from. Nearby houses didn't have any. They were not part of the lot design, but believe me, all different shapes and sizes were scattered everywhere.

"Welcome, looking for anything specific?" a woman asked.

I assume the woman greeting me was Pebbles. She wore a black apron wrapped around her white oxford shirt with black slacks.

"Are you Pebbles?" I asked for validation.

"Yes, I am. What can I help you with?" she questioned.

"I'd like to check out some options for hair weave," I spilled my plan, not that I had a beautician in mind to sew in the weave.

"Come this way," Pebbles said as she ushered me towards the back of the store.

I really preferred to just look around.

After being shown about ten options, I felt overwhelmed and decided I'd just get a wig. I found one that had a part down the center. It hung down on the sides with a slight flare outward. It was simple and about my hair length…gave me a fuller look.

"I like," Pebbles complimented.

Something told me she'd like anything I tried.

"Thank you, I'll take this one," I replied.

My patience hadn't made it to its high point yet, but I just couldn't see being in a hair store longer than twenty minutes trying on various pieces others had already tried on. *Ugh!*

I decided I'd wear my new hair out the store. Pebbles threw in a hair net. For some reason, I thought I could just slap on my wig and go. Growing up, Willie Mae used to emphasize how learning was ongoing. Every day I learned something new. I didn't know if the net was to help the wig stay on, or if it was to help minimize the itching. I just learned it belonged between my head and the wig.

As I guided my hands through my purse, blindly swiping for my keys, the tune of "This is the Day" sounded from my cell phone. Passing by my keys, I grabbed my phone. Isaac's number appeared on the caller ID. *Weird! He never called during his work hours.*

"Hello Boo Bear," I answered in my sexy voice.

"Evette, this is Benjamin. I have Isaac's phone. I am taking him to the hospital. He's okay…not trying to scare you. A tree fell on him and shook him up pretty badly," Benjamin explained in one long sentence failing to catch his breath.

Freaked out…back to fumbling for my keys, I cried out, "Oh my, I'll meet you there!"

"Okay, I will be taking him to St. Matthew's Hospital," Benjamin shared.

Thank God, I wouldn't have known which hospital; I didn't know where they had been.

According to the doctor with no name badge, Isaac had suffered from a concussion. He diagnosed him based off the information provided by Benjamin. Even though I had no medical background, I wasn't impressed by "Doctor No Badge." No badge meant no knowledge in my eyes. He decided to keep Isaac a few hours, anticipating a dismissal to follow. Unfortunately, it was time to pick the kids up from school. I didn't want to leave Isaac's side. Ms. Joyce Ann was gone before I left the house. More than likely she was unavailable. Feeling stuck, I had no choice...

"Benjamin, would you mind picking up the kids from school? You can bring them here. It would help me out so much!" I asked, begging at the same time.

"Sure, I will be happy to pick them up. No problem at all. Is there anything else I can do?"

It was sweet of him to ask.

"On the way back, if you can stop to get them a small snack, that will be awesome. Be sure to get you something as well," I said, handing over twenty dollars.

"I don't know that I'll need anything, but I will definitely get the kids something," Benjamin replied.

Such a sweet man. What woman wouldn't want him?

Isaac had fallen asleep. I was told I shouldn't allow him to drift off when he got home. Kinda strange, they didn't mind him drifting off in the hospital. Lord knows my boo was too sexy to have any injuries, especially to that smooth, dark complexioned face. No scratches on his body. God is good!

"Thank You, Lord, for keeping *my* Isaac free of major injuries. I ask that he fully recovers. Thank You for placing Benjamin in our lives. Please bless him in all he does. Amen," I prayed.

Isaac had picked up Benjamin for the day. Afraid to leave him home alone, I instructed Benjamin to keep the truck a day until we could figure out a way to have it picked up. By the time we arrived home, Isaac was back in his right state of mind. He tried romancing me at bedtime. I instructed him to rest up before I hit him in the head again. No matter the situation, one of us managed to squeeze in a little humor from time to time. Eventually, he drifted off. It was not like I could lay there and hold his eyes open, so I wasn't sure how I was supposed to keep him awake. Instead, I fought to keep my eyes open most of the night. I may have gotten about two hours of sleep.

The following day was Saturday. Of course, it was Isaac's weekend to have Shantel. Not trying to avoid the company, but I advised Isaac to discuss his circumstance with Quintella to let her know he needed to pass up on his weekend. It was the first time he couldn't keep Shantel since birth. I assumed Quintella understood. I didn't ask. I only had something to say if she had refused. Isaac went about the house as usual, but I forced him to stay home another day. Benjamin had another greeter from the church follow him over to drop off Isaac's truck. It was returned in one piece, which is what I would have expected, no worries.

Later that evening, the kids requested to watch a family movie. There was a new Annie movie out that I hadn't seen that starred Jamie Foxx. I must say, I was not one who cared for musicals, but this remake had me glued to the screen. A great family movie with no uncomfortable, close your eyes scenes. I guess it would have been okay for Shantel to stay over, but it was too late to reverse the plan. Besides, it was possible we would have not had Singleton quality time having her over. I loved Shantel with all my heart, but the kids seemed to be more at ease when she wasn't present. They deserved their own separate family time. Life was more hectic during the week, so, what better time to spend quality time as a family than the weekend. Especially the entire day.

Destiny Who?

Michelle Lee, thirty-eight weeks into pregnancy, was preparing for her special delivery. One Tuesday at approximately nine o'clock in the morning, Quintella phoned Isaac, asking if he was available to pick up Shantel. It was not his agreed day. Isaac told his customer he needed to swing by his baby's mama's to pick up his daughter and he'd return momentarily. He meant what he said alright. He swung by to pick up Shantel; he also swung by the house to drop her off for *me* to babysit. I considered it an even trade, favor for favor. Isaac couldn't pick up Shantel on one of his days; he ended up picking her up on a day that wasn't his. Fair call.

Benjamin rushed to the hospital as well. I could only hope he wouldn't be shoved out of the room while Quintella and Michelle Lee worked through the birthing process. I sure hated he had to be involved with Michelle Lee out of all classmates. Why not Chasity Gregory or Lorna Nixon? I didn't care for them either, but at least they were not my enemy. Between Isaac and me, Quintella and

191

Michelle Lee, and then Benjamin, I felt we were all wrapped up in a big love-hate triangle. The sad part, it was not something that would ever go away. No crime had been committed, but the punishment we were serving was a life sentence. We would be together forever!

Shantel was asleep on arrival. Dirty on awakening. Fussy after a diaper change. Busy after fed. Eleven months to the fullest, her bowlegs attempted steps. She was flopping down all over the place. Times as such made me wish Isaac had bought a swing set or something. Trust me, she would have been fastened in. What was more special than one on one time with my stepdaughter? It didn't seem to faze Quintella; she was tied up in the stepchild to come.

Several hours had passed. Back to my early parental days, I buckled Shantel into her car seat and fastened her in the back of the SUV. It was time to pick up the kids. I didn't think I'd have her that long. I guess I forgot labor didn't mean speedy delivery. I was in labor with Danielle for eight hours before she finally decided to work her way to the preferred position, head down. JaRon came within two hours. I barely made it to the hospital with Isaac Jr. He popped out like he had somewhere to be.

"Where's Daddy?" Danielle asked as she hopped into the back with Shantel.

"Is today our day?" Isaac Jr. asked.

He was one to share information. I was surprised he questioned the day. He knew Tuesday was not the typical schedule. JaRon hopped in, booty bumping Danielle to the center. For once, he didn't have any questions. There was always one child who chose to avoid questions. It was like they secretly played a my turn not to ask game.

"Daddy is at work. Shantel's mother had something come up. She needed him to pick her up today. So no, Jr., today is not our day." I said, answering two questions in one.

The kids had no clue of the other life outside of Shantel.

Back home, I threw some cold-cuts together and issued the kids a bag of Cheetos, telling them the combination would have to do for the day. I fed Shantel a little jar of Gerber carrots and handed her a half bottle of formula. She was able to hold her own. Realizing I never ate breakfast or lunch, I quickly threw together a sandwich for me and grabbed a bag of chips. Feeling every bit of my age, I was ready for Isaac to return.

Evidently, Benjamin had my number locked in *his* cell phone as well. He called to share that his little girl, Destiny, was born. She weighed nine pounds, eight ounces. I wanted to ask questions. I refrained. *Was he allowed to witness the birth? Did Destiny have his last name? Would he be listed on the birth certificate?*

"Lord not my business," I said to myself.

He sounded like a proud dad. I asked if the baby had any hair, trying to find out anything I could. He said she had a head full of black shiny hair and long toes. At first, I thought I heard long nose, but the "t" sound was noted. He added she was chubby and beautiful as can be. I wondered if he knew Michelle Lee was plump in high school. I didn't feel the need to share. Again, it was then I knew I was a changed woman. I took time to think before I spoke. Yes...I had changed alright.

I congratulated Benjamin on his little girl. I asked if Isaac had been notified. He hadn't called Isaac yet. I was surprised. He wanted me to have the news first. I didn't know if I should be honored or what. *He thought of me first!* All I could do was congratulate him again. I told him I'd check with Isaac once he returned to see if he had heard the news. I was beginning to conclude we'd have Shantel longer than I imagined. Wednesday was our usual day, so I couldn't see her going home just to return the following morning. *When would Michelle Lee be discharged?* Oh my, babysitter reality was kicking in!

Isaac returned later than his usual. He ended up working alone and got behind on time.

"Benjamin had a little girl," he said after bending over to kiss me on the forehead.

"He called me," I replied.

"Oh, he did? Okay..." Isaac said with a little hesitancy.

"Yeah, I guess he knew you were busy, I don't know," I tried to provide rationale.

Isaac explained the plan was for Benjamin to sign the birth certificate, but Michelle Lee wanted the baby to have either her last name or Quintella's. That was a new one for me.

"So, I guess her name is Destiny Who," I said trying to incorporate a little humor.

Isaac grinned while peeking in at Shantel who had fallen asleep, looking like she had behaved all day. He kissed the kids and headed straight to the shower. I apologized for the cold-cuts and chips, but it was what it was.

Mutual Agreement

"Good morning, Benjamin. Come on in. How are you?" I greeted, invited, and asked.

"Good morning, Evette. I can't complain," Benjamin responded.

"Isaac already left for work. He has been going out about an hour earlier since he doesn't have your help now," I explained.

"How is daddy life?" I asked.

"Wonderful…never thought I'd produce such a beautiful little baby girl," Benjamin responded.

Benjamin stopped by to tell Isaac he would be taking off for a while. Evidently, Quintella and Michelle Lee agreed he could stay in their spare room for a few weeks to help with Destiny. I could tell right off he was being used, but I didn't want to stir up anything. *Why was he so gullible?*

Instead of opening his eyes like Sophia and Ms. Joyce Ann opened mine, I tried another approach hoping eventually he'd see for himself. I explained he was a good man who deserved nothing but the best. I commended him on being such a reliable work partner for Isaac and just being available to help with the kids when we needed.

Using words of encouragement, I informed Benjamin he would find himself someone one day who would really appreciate him. I assured him I understood his struggles and his efforts to do what was right, even though he was not always rewarded fairly. Evidently, I hit a nerve. Benjamin put his chin down to his chest. At first, I thought he was praying. It only took a second to realize he was shedding tears.

"Evette, you don't understand how hard I have tried. I make it because I give all my problems to the good Lord every day," he expressed while pouting.

Like me, Benjamin knew to give credit to God.

I placed my hand on Benjamin's balled fist, hoping to alleviate some of his tension. I consumed his pain, but not without noticing the scent of some cologne he had on. He smelled good, so good my hand magically eased up to his arms. I rubbed them. Then, I kneeled beside him. Caught up in the moment, Benjamin stood up. He pulled me back up. We embraced. Immediately our eyes connected. Our heads mutually approached each other until reality hit; we were about to commit a sin. Before our lips could connect, I backed away.

"I am so sorry," I apologized.

Frozen from guilt, we stood there a minute.

"Well, Evette, I guess I better go. I have so much respect for Isaac; I must leave now," Benjamin explained.

"I don't know what just happened, but yes, it may be a good time to leave," I agreed.

Benjamin moped towards the door.

"Hey Benji...Isaac doesn't have to know about this, okay? Nothing happened so let's leave it be. Please," I begged.

"Yes ma'am," Benjamin approved.

I never knew the main reason for the visit. He said he dropped by to inform Isaac he'd be taking off for a while. As far as I was concerned, he could have called him for that. One thing about it, I saw how easy it could be to get wrapped up in a moment. I liked Benjamin. I felt like we had a unique connection. It was like we had a deep understanding of each other's current and past pains. He understood me. I understood him. He had empathy. I had empathy. I stood in the door as he drove away as though I didn't want to see him go.

I called him Benji! Where did that come from?

It was one odd start to the day. The experience was indeed a secret I had to keep. I didn't want to ruin his work opportunities.

I wondered if Isaac at least had some physical connection with Quintella during his affair. No doubt, I felt vibes with Benjamin. I hate to admit it, but let the truth be known, I was beginning to think about him often. I couldn't see him with Sophia. They clashed. I just wanted to see him happy with someone. Isaac could have anyone he wanted. But on the other hand, poor old Benjamin was getting mistreated and taken for granted. Life was full of curve balls.

"Lord please erase what just happened. I love Isaac. I do not want anything to come between us. Forgive me. Please place someone in Benjamin's life who will appreciate him and love him for the man he is. Amen," I prayed.

I figured Isaac didn't need to know about the visit period. I wouldn't have known what to share anyway. As much as I wanted Isaac to stop keeping secrets from me, my little once in a lifetime slip up was not going to be revealed...at least not by me.

Isaac came home later that evening. The day went on as usual. I was good; a little fidgety, but good. Isaac was good. The kids were good, up to their usual routines. When bedtime came, I made sure to allow Isaac to fall asleep first. I would not have wanted to fall asleep and speak out my potential affair in a dream. I knew once Isaac was out, he wouldn't hear anything if I were to talk out the day.

I laid there in awe, still thinking about Benjamin and what had happened. I wondered what it would be like seeing him in Isaac's presence. *Would he feel uncomfortable? Would I feel uncomfortable?*

The almost affair was eating at me…I felt maybe our little close call should not be kept a secret after all; but, then those nerves of mine, being my advocate, spoke up for me and said, "Oh no, keep it secret Evette, keep it secret, don't do it sista!"

A secret it was!

Birthday Dilemma

The kids' birthdays had already come and gone. We promised to take them on a special family vacation. That would be our way to celebrate them all. Things had been so discombobulated the past year or so. Danielle's birthday had just passed. JaRon's birthday passed in January. Isaac Jr.'s birthday was last November. As parents, we failed when it came to acknowledging birthdays. Well, actually we missed Isaac Jr.'s. We felt it would only be fair to not celebrate the remaining two. We sat the kids down and promised a family vacation to Disney World...*You know, the place of la la land where I commonly found myself.*

Baby Shantel was going from zero to hero. One day from turning one. Quintella invited Isaac over for the party. Yes, that was a problem! The things that do not cross your mind ahead of time. There were a lot of things I didn't like already. The birthday situation took the cake. I didn't feel Isaac needed to attend the party at Quintella's

203

house, just like I would have never invited Quintella to attend a party at ours. Every single time I tried to get closer to God, a test would follow. *Why me?*

Isaac didn't see anything wrong with stopping by Quintella's for the party. Typical of him. Non-confrontational. If that were the case, then I felt the kids should have been invited as well. Who cared they were older? They were half brothers and sister! I didn't want to pray about this one. I wanted to have full control over the outcome. After Quintella and Michelle Lee ran game on me with the grocery store and phone call incidences, I didn't trust them one lick. Especially after I saw the game they were playing on Benjamin. In my opinion, they put the "scandal" in scandalous.

"Why can't we just have our own party here?" I asked Isaac.

"Baby we can have a party here. I would love to celebrate here as well. Now, Evette, I don't see anything wrong with me swinging by for the party. I can take the kids. I shouldn't have to ask if they can come. If anything, I can at least take Danielle," Isaac gave his two cents.

"Well, I am not liking it one bit. Either all three will go or none of them will. Sorry to be a party pooper, but that is how I feel. If we have a party here, I don't see why you must go there and be all up in their house," I argued.

"Evette, you sure make it hard. Shantel is my daughter, and just like I support my kids here, I want to support my daughter there as well. It will be okay. I will take the kids and we will just stay for a short period. Let's leave it at that," Isaac said, putting down his foot in a polite manner.

Did the knucklehead just check me? So, he's going? My opinion didn't matter!

"Whatever!" I shouted.

Hell, I didn't have anything else to say. Isaac pretty much told me he was going. For the first time the dude demonstrated he had a little backbone.

I had a strong feeling if I continued to push the issue, my non-confrontational husband would have become confrontational. If anything, I grasped he loved Shantel just as much as he did Danielle, JaRon, and Isaac Jr. I realized this would not be the first time. More birthdays would come. Baptisms…possibly. Graduations. All the things I didn't consider ahead of time. I finally got used to Shantel and her ways. Then it hit me, I had to get used to Quintella and her ways too!

What happens when daycare is needed? What happens when school starts?

"Lord, where art Thou?" I asked.

Morning came. The party was scheduled for two o'clock. The kids were going. Isaac Jr. and JaRon really didn't care to go. I encouraged them to be supportive of their half-sister. Really, I wanted to have more control over the situation and to have extra eyes on the happenings. We agreed the party would continue at our place at five o'clock. The only guest from the *other* house invited to our party was Benjamin. We didn't even include Destiny. Well…I didn't. I felt it was fair to invite Benjamin since he helped with the kids. Plus, it would get him away from being used over Michelle Lee's and Quintella's. I invited Ms. Joyce Ann, Sophia, and Gina and her little ones. We hadn't met them yet. I figured it would be a good time to invite them. I didn't invite Gina's nephew, but I would have been okay if he came.

While Isaac and the kids were getting their party on elsewhere, I made a quick run to the grocery store. I saw Sophia was about to head to the mini mart. I asked if she wanted to ride with me to the store instead. That was a first. She jumped in; the right side of the car tilting downward. What better conversation to have than about Benjamin? Without hesitation, I asked Sophia if she could see herself with Benjamin. I explained how I thought he was being taken for granted and used. Sophia had never thought about it. She reminded me that he did flirt with her from time to time, but she never took him seriously. She claimed she was so used to living alone and having her own privacy. *Privacy was an interesting word choice.* If he were to come on to her; however, she said she'd consider.

By no means was I a relationship match person, but that was all I needed to hear. I had to come up with a way to see if Benjamin was interested in Sophia. Sophia was different and had her own style, but I couldn't see her using him, even with her handicap. Who knows, maybe they both just needed someone to talk to and share life experiences. She was the best choice I could come up with. I was married. Ms. Joyce Ann was too old. Gina was married. I couldn't think of any former co-workers.

"Good deal," I thought.

I told Sophia I was getting ready to decorate for the party. I also explained Shantel would be having two parties. I finally asked Sophia for her two cents. I figured, why not? I asked if it was right for Isaac to go over to Quintella's. As much as I wanted her to agree with my thoughts, she assured me Isaac did the correct thing.

Darn it!

She had the nerves to flip the script. She asked me, "If the shoe were on the other foot, what would you expect?"

I imagined having a baby by Benjamin. I was asked to go to his house to celebrate our baby's first birthday even though I was married to Isaac. Yes, I could see where I would have wanted to go. It just took positioning me in the situation to finally see that it was a reasonable expectation.

I stopped by the bakery. I picked out a little Winnie the Pooh cake. Since Isaac had gotten Shantel the Winnie the Pooh bouncer, it was the first cake to catch my eye. I pulled one yellow balloon and one white one from the balloon rack to coordinate. With the same hand, I grabbed a #1 candle from the candle display. As I headed to the ice-cream aisle, I realized my hands were too full to grab the eight pack of vanilla ice-cream cups. Sophia was nowhere in sight. I figured I'd have the sacker go back to get them. That was the least he could do. Otherwise service sucked as usual. I decided the ice cream and cake was enough. There was no need to get a lot of food if they were going to be eating at the first stop. I wanted to get just enough to acknowledge the moment. Plus, I didn't know if Gina and the kids would swing by or not. Kids can be picky. I didn't want to worry about having too much.

Sophia had grabbed a few things for herself. She was waiting on me at the bench located at the front of the store. I didn't think I took long to grab what I needed, but she had already made her way around. Upon checking out, I realized I had forgotten a tablecloth. I didn't go back. When *my* kids had their first party, I didn't go all out of the way, so what I had was gonna have to work.

Isaac and the kids returned after an hour.

"Where's Shantel?" I asked.

Isaac said Quintella never agreed Shantel could come back to our house. It was Thursday.

"You mean to tell me we have to wait until Saturday to celebrate after I have invited the entire block! Did you bother to press the matter?" I questioned, raising my voice from frustration.

Sophia excused herself. She said she'd check back later. Funny, she was nosey from across the way; she had an opportunity to be dead center in the action and she excused herself.

"Evette, I didn't push the issue. Let's just put the cake in the refrigerator and put the ice cream in the freezer. I will walk down to let Gina know to come by Saturday. Then, I will stop by Ms. Joyce Ann's. It's going to be okay; I promise baby. Thank you for all you've done. I see your hard work," Isaac thoroughly communicated for once, trying to wear the britches again.

I had it! I marched past the kids and headed straight to the bedroom. Not only did I slam the door, but also, I locked the darn thing! I felt like I was being treated as a kid. Isaac was talking to me as though I was the baby. I didn't appreciate it. I admit, I may have been having a temper tantrum moment, but I was not the darn problem. I freakin' gave in to him going over there, busted my butt trying to set up things at our house, just to be rejected because it wasn't our day. Isaac bent over backward for her ass. The bitch didn't want to bend over backward for his. Hell, it was the girl's birthday, for goodness sake! Yes, I resumed back to cussing. Enough was enough!

"Lord I am done. I can't win for losing!" I screamed to the top of my lungs.

Broken Promises

No matter what happened the previous night, sista girl slept without any problems. Isaac slept in the recliner in the living room. Never in ten years had I ever locked the bedroom door. I am no fool though, I know he could have gotten in if he wanted. At first, I tried to get mad because he didn't attempt to come to bed. After speaking with myself, I let it go. As usual, Isaac had the kids off to school and had left for work. There was no breakfast on the table for me. At first, I tried to get mad because he didn't bother to cook for me. After speaking with myself, I let that go too. Between the two of us, one of us was tripping. I was bound to find out who.

I decided I would seclude myself inside the house. I forced myself to read my Bible. They say the closer you are to God, the more would be revealed through reading. Well sista needed to get a little bit closer. However, I really didn't grasp the Word for the day. Nothing was on television. Nothing exciting appeared to be going on from my window view. Sophia was out reciting. I didn't want to interfere with her routine. Ms. Joyce Ann had cars lined in the driveway and on the curb. She was holding her knitting class. No sight of Gina.

Bored as bored could be, I decided I'd check the kid's closets to see if all was in order. I routinely cleaned out clothes every six months. It didn't take long for them to outgrow their clothes, especially Danielle. She was growing like a weed. Lucky me, their clothes were good for another six-month round. I decided I'd wash everyone's bedding. Now, that was a shame; I couldn't recall the last time I did. I grabbed Shantel's crib sheet and blanket. After clearing her crib, I begin to reminisce back to the prior day. Even though she was not the primary blame, I did believe she played a part in our problems. Perhaps indirectly. Isaac's sin led to family problems we never had in the past. *Was our marriage doomed?*

All I could think about was what if I had cheated? Where would we be? What if Benjamin and I kissed and it led to other things? I had my tubes tied back in the day, so a baby wouldn't have been a possible outcome. Would Isaac have stayed with me? I felt like I was hanging in there, even though I was wronged. How would I know if he would have hung in there if he was wronged? I'd been through thick and thin. Would he have endured thick and thin? I am sure Dr. Gregg would have said we both had been through thick and thin. One thing I was beginning to hate about marriage was the "two becoming one" part. No, he did what he did. I should not have had to suffer because of his unfaithfulness.

I began to doubt my marriage. My bad days were beginning to outweigh my good days. Some of the reasoning could have been my fault but I didn't care. I loved Isaac. Isaac needed to have loved me the same. *Why come he couldn't fight the temptation? Why come he couldn't push away like Benjamin and I did? His ass gave in. He had consensual sex with Quintella. Baby Shantel was not a mistake!*

Isaac came home early. School was still in session. He caught me off guard. I had just finished showering. I had a late start. As I was exiting the bathroom, Isaac was entering the bedroom.

"Hey," he spoke to me as we locked eyes.

"Hey," I replied as I attempted to brush past him to the dresser drawer.

Isaac grabbed my arm, which was a first.

"Evette, I got off early today because we need to talk," he enlightened.

"I don't know that we have anything to talk about. You pretty much are doing what you want, so it is what it is," I said.

Letting go of my arm, Isaac yelled, **"You know you can be a butt sometimes yourself Evette! I made a mistake, I thought we were working through this. You are making it harder than it has to be! I don't want Quintella, but I will take care of my child! You knew that before I returned. What do you want from me now?"**

A sista didn't know what the hell to think.

"First of all, don't be pulling on my arm! Second of all, you knew I could be a 'butt' when you married me. It was cute! Remember? Third of all, I expect you to take care of your damn child! I didn't expect you to have another one, but yes, I expect you to take care of your child!" I yelled back.

"Well, Evette I cheated! Accept it. I cheated! Now what?" Isaac continued with an elevated voice.

My husband was now confrontational. He literally raised his voice at me for the first time in our marriage. I saw he was upset.

"Well…just so you know, I almost cheated…"

I paused. This was supposed to be a secret! Oops!

Well, whatever, I decided to throw it out there.

"I almost cheated on your ass the other day. Yeah that's right. Benjamin came over for whatever reason and we talked. We were about to kiss. I at least had the guts to pull apart. I loved you enough to not let it happen. So how do you feel about that?" I asked, deciding to lower my voice a notch.

"Oh really, so now you got game. That's why you wanted him to babysit the kids, huh? So, you're better than me because you resisted? I didn't cheat on you in our house! You had another man over in our house. Maybe the two of you should have screwed! Maybe you would have felt even since you like to be so

214

revengeful all the time. You know what Evette, whatever…I will just sleep on the sofa until you figure out what you want. I will let you explain to the kids. You're too hard to please! If you want Benjamin, so be it. I don't need another man helping me who wants to screw my wife!" Isaac continued to yell.

I spent the next thirty minutes or so trying to explain that Benjamin was not trying to screw me. I asked Isaac not to mention the matter to Benjamin. For one, I had broken the promise. For two, I knew I wasn't going to allow an affair to happen. I knew Benjamin had no intentions on hurting Isaac. I figured I owed Benjamin enough to assure his job with Isaac wasn't affected. I literally begged Isaac not to say anything. In fact, I begged him to understand. I told him everything. I had let go of the baby situation. I wanted Isaac to understand the Benjamin situation.

"I guess I will head to pick up the kids. Carry on," Isaac said rudely, cutting me off.

He simply walked out the room. The knucklehead literally left. One thing for sure, he had leaving a sista hanging mastered. I had no clue what was going on in his mind.

Isaac argued with me. He had never argued. I was shocked! It could not be happening.

What was going on? Was I tripping?

He pulled me by my arm! He didn't do so abusively, but still—he pulled me by my arm! I was so stunned; it took a minute for me to realize I never got my undies from the dresser. I stood there naked. This time without three kids staring.

Dual Counsel

I had no idea how to move forward in my marriage. Everything was out of hand. I don't think the kids were aware of the magnitude of the problems that existed. I mean, they may have seen bits and pieces of disagreements, but nothing drastic to where they questioned. There were no changes in their behavior at home. None at school reported. That was good. They didn't deserve to be caught up in the middle of me and Isaac's trials and tribulations.

Isaac headed to pick up the kids from school. I placed a call to Dr. Gregg. I explained the latest. She felt it would be best for me to see if Isaac would join for a session. I knew things had to be serious. I had seen her about a year. She never asked me to check to see if Isaac would like to accompany me. Our problems were maxed. I never spoke the divorce word to Isaac, but I had spoken it several times to Dr. Gregg. Interestingly so, I had reached a point where I could have cared less about the house. As far as I was concerned, Isaac could have it all. I was willing to start over!

We somehow managed to fake it through the weekend for the sake of the kids. Shantel had her little cake and ice-cream gathering. Sophia returned. I was waiting on her to ask for an update since she knew there were issues. She didn't ask anything. She and Benjamin were carrying on some conversation. It looked too good to interrupt. I couldn't tell if Isaac had said anything to Benjamin. Everything seemed cool between the two. For once, I acted as normal as I could.

Ms. Joyce Ann came. She made Shantel the cutest little sweater. It was all pink, made of crochet. She said she made it for her to wear to church. Lord knows, I didn't know the next time we'd attend. Gina came with her two kids. They were a pleasure to meet. She had a nine-year-old son and an eleven-year-old daughter. She had picked up Shantel a little Cabbage Patch doll. It had been a long time since I had seen one of those. It didn't look new, but it was decent. Maybe she was a thrifty shopper or maybe she handed down one of her daughter's dolls. It was the thought that counted. Her nephew did not accompany them. I could only wish he didn't feel left out. The kids had a ball. They made up their own games around the house.

Isaac and I only spoke when it was necessary. We were respectful to one another but nothing extra. No pats on the butt, no kisses. No nothing! After the party, everyone went their own ways. I spoke to Benjamin when he came in. I didn't want to find myself in an awkward moment with him, so I kept my distance. I spoke to him again when he left with Sophia. They seem to have had some more talking to do. I was cool with that. Shantel was winding down. Isaac

218

went to put her to bed, then came back to the living room. The kids decided they would play Uno. So, that left me and Isaac sitting around looking pitiful.

I asked Isaac to meet me in the bedroom. He complied. We both sat on the edge of the bed about five inches apart. I could feel the tension. I told him I had called Dr. Gregg. I had planned to see her the following Monday. I mentioned she asked if he would like to attend. I felt obligated to say our marriage was on the rocks and I felt counseling was the only intervention left to try to save it. I even offered a different counselor if Isaac wanted to try another person, being that Dr. Gregg had only known one side of the story from day one.

"Evette, I imagine I can squeeze it in. It will have to be during my lunch hour...now, you know, I pretty much have a set schedule. I imagine Benjamin can drive the truck, and I can take the car so he can continue on if I am late getting back," Isaac carried on and on, at least willing to give it a try.

"Do you want to go? Or are you just going?" I asked.

"Evette, if it is something that can help us, I am willing to give it a try. I've told you over and over again that I love you. I don't know what else to say or do at this point," Isaac explained.

"Okay, Isaac, I love you too. I will call her Monday morning and see if we can come in the afternoon. If not, we can shoot for the afternoon hour on Tuesday," I replied.

"Okay," Isaac said.

Isaac stood up; he looked into my eyes. I saw the shame. He positioned himself in front of me and kissed me on the cheek before exiting the bedroom. Through it all, he still had some compassion left in his heart. I sat there a while, shed a few tears, and back to praying I went.

"Lord, the devil is working me. I rebuke the devil in Your name. I need Isaac. Isaac needs me. The kids need us. Please let counseling reunite us. Yes, we are in the same household, but we are still divided. I ask in Your Son's name, please fix our marriage. Please! Amen," I cried some more.

Crying was beginning to be a routine for me. I was thankful I didn't wear makeup every day. I'd sure hate to fix all up just for it to be ruined. Hmm…maybe the brand I used was cheap. Perhaps, make-up wearers wore high dollar makeup. I sat there until Isaac returned to ask me to join him and the kids for a movie. Shantel was still asleep. I complied.

Monday came. Dr. Gregg was able to squeeze us in for the afternoon. I met Isaac at her office. The first session was quick. She just asked us if we loved one another and only wanted a "yes" or "no" answer.

Then, she asked if we wanted our marriage to work and expected the same, just a "yes" or "no" answer. We passed! She gave us an assignment to work on and asked if we would be willing to see her every Monday for three additional weeks. We agreed.

The first week our assignment consisted of jotting down all the qualities we admired about each other. We were not to share our lists. She asked us to only focus on positives. She didn't ask us to jot down the things we disliked; she must have known my list would have been longer. Then again, maybe Isaac had things he had kept to himself throughout the years and he would have surprised me.

The following Monday we discussed the list. She had us read our list to each other. Isaac liked I was a faithful wife, a good mother, and I made every effort to be pleasing in God's sight. He liked I could cook, I was beautiful, and I was just a hard worker in general. My list was pretty much similar. I liked he could cook. I put I had just recently learned that. That was my humor moment for the day. I expressed he was a hard worker and loved his kids. Of course, I added he was handsome. Dr. Gregg had to validate if I felt Isaac was a good husband. She only expected a "yes" or a "no."

I replied, "Yes."

According to Dr. Gregg, without knowing anything else, she had no doubt Isaac, and I would endure our problems. She assured us our assignment proved we had the most important qualities. I couldn't add

221

he didn't communicate the best. She wasn't looking for any negatives. That would have been first on my list of negatives if allowed.

Our next assignment was for us to spend at least one hour a day alone without the kids, or any interruptions. She wanted us to take one quality from our list each day and initiate a conversation regarding it. Once again, she emphasized to only stick to positives. She was making it hard on a sista, but I trusted her. She had the degree; I didn't.

Isaac and I were able to spend seven hours together out of the one hundred and sixty-eight hours over the week. We did as we were advised. Amazingly so, a few of the nights led to some good make-up sex. The passion was still there for sure. I was beginning to see the point. My good days had dwindled down, but Isaac's good qualities outweighed his bad. It was not about the days; it was about the qualities. We could rebuild based off the qualities. I felt brave enough to bring my thoughts to Isaac's attention. He expressed on the other hand, that his good days with me had not dwindled below the bad, and my good qualities outweighed the bad as well. What I learned was he didn't hold me to the same standards I held him to. The higher the standards the more disappointments. In other words, he was more flexible.

Dr. Gregg was pleased. We were getting exactly what she intended from the sessions. She explained many people dwell on the negatives so much, they are weighed down when the negatives are a smaller percent. She pointed out it was like the "grass is greener on the other side" belief. The grass is not any greener on the other side. Isaac and I just needed to nurture our side more.

Our final assignment was to take a family vacation with the kids. What she didn't know is we had planned one. We had some birthday making up to do with the kids. After I brought it to her attention, she strongly advised for us to stick with the plan. One exception, she wanted Shantel to be included.

Dr. Gregg looked me dead in the eyes and said, "Shantel is 100% part of the family though only 50% of the blood. She is to be loved the same and included as much as possible in all milestone events."

Dr. Gregg looked at Isaac directly in the eyes and said "Quintella cannot depict what events you attend and what events you can't. There should be no event you attend that your wife or kids are not equally invited. If an event should rise where your wife or kids are not invited, then it is not one you should attend."

She expressed he didn't even have to debate or explain himself to Quintella. She called it "conditioning." She said Quintella would get it.

At the end of our last session, Dr. Gregg prayed for our marriage. One thing I liked about her was she was a praying counselor. She asked us the same questions from day one. Our answers were still "yes." She then said to take what we had learned and expand off it. She said to leave out the negatives. She wanted us to agree to hold each other accountable of staying positive. She said if so, eventually the negatives would cure itself.

I didn't have to bring up Quintella anymore. I didn't have to answer about my close affair with Benjamin. Isaac knew he had to set boundaries with Quintella for the sake of his marriage. It was like neither of us needed to point the finger. We just needed to do what was best for us individually so we could come together to do what was best for the family.

I trusted the situation so much that sista girl literally went home, opened the medicine cabinet, and poured out my Lexapro. It was like releasing balloons at a significant event. I released relying on medications to fix me. I wanted to fix myself. That night Isaac and I made love like we did at his apartment. A sista was back on her grind every night as before. Isaac was *my* Boo Bear. I had *my* dream man back, in full effect!

Family Vacation

Finally, the Singleton family vacation was about to go down. Quintella okayed for Isaac to keep Shantel Wednesday thru Monday. Therefore, we used the allotted privilege to book our vacation. I must say, I was proud of my Boo Bear. He had followed the recommendations of Dr. Gregg. There were a couple times Quintella wanted Isaac to participate in milestone moments, but Isaac handled it well. One situation was when Shantel was christened. She invited Isaac. He told her we would *all* be there. That was that. We went. We sat together. We took pictures and we came home. Another situation was when Shantel had to go to the doctor for a fever. We met Quintella at the doctor's office. The kids and I remained in the lobby while Isaac went back. He came out. We went home. If anything, his consistency showed Quintella there would be no game allowed.

Another summer had come. School was out. There was no need for camp because I no longer worked. Isaac had saved up money for our family vacation. Shantel was now fourteen months. Danielle was eight years old. JaRon was ten years old. Isaac Jr. was one year away from being a teenager. To add, Isaac and I were both thirty-one years of age. Despite anyone's age, we concluded no one was too old to go to Disney World! We asked the kids if the vacation would break us even on the birthdays. They all yelled *yes* at the top of their lungs. I had never seen such a level of excitement in our three bears.

Everyone was packed. Isaac had purchased the vacation package. Tickets were in hand. We picked up Shantel at 4:30 am and hurried to the airport to catch our flight. For whatever reason we had to be there at least two hours early. We had taken several road trips, but this was our first time flying. I was nervous and thrilled at the same time. I was with my family. We were all happy. This vacation was the most meaningful vacation since we tied the knot. If anything, it was indeed the biggest one!

I fully accepted Shantel as my own. My love for her had grown so much just because I loved her dad so much. Diaper changing became natural to me. She was still drinking from a bottle longer than I would have expected, but assuring her thirst was quenched had become routine of me. She no longer drank formula. Instead, she had advanced to two percent milk and a selection of juices. I had patience with fussy moments. She no longer stressed me.

The kids were awed at the sight of the airport.

"Mom are we going to be on a plane like that?" Danielle asked, pointing to a plane that had just taken off.

226

"Yes, baby we will be on one very similar," I replied.

"Wow," JaRon commented.

"Welcome to the Singleton Family Vacation," Isaac announced as though he was the pilot of the plane we had not yet boarded.

"This is going to be fun," Isaac Jr. joined the conversation.

"Yes, it is," I responded.

We were expected to arrive in Florida by noon. The kids were unaware our hotel would be right in the center of all the action. Isaac booked a resort that would knock the kids off their feet. My Boo Bear's taste was exceptional. I forgot to put that on my list of good qualities; I am not sure how I left that off.

We decided we'd hang around the resort the first night and settle in. We planned to visit the theme park Thursday and Friday. On Saturday, the plan was to hop on and off the shuttle so the kids could have multiple experiences. We didn't know where we'd go, we figured we'd play it by ear or ask around when the time came. Isaac had already said he'd carry Shantel when needed. He knew she would not always be in the mood to walk. He pre-informed me he wanted me to enjoy the vacation in its entirety.

We boarded the plane first class. The kids were bouncing all over the place; even Isaac Jr. at age twelve. I had to take a few deep breaths to remind myself I was an adult. I wanted to bounce all over the place as well.

"This is humongous!" JaRon yelled.

"Yes, this is humongous!" Danielle mocked JaRon.

"I know I won't be going to sleep," Isaac Jr. said.

"Me either," both Danielle and JaRon agreed.

The kids sat in the seats in front of Isaac, Shantel, and me. We figured Isaac Jr. could have the luxury of the window seat since his birthday had been the first one neglected. Also, he was the photographer. Danielle sat in the middle, leaving JaRon on the aisle end. He didn't seem to mind. They could all see out the window. We figured if there were any problems, they could switch on the return home.

The flight attendants took their positions, demonstrated safety techniques, and explained the emergency exits. Danielle led us in a quick prayer. The kids were showered with drinks of their choice. Shantel was awake and calm with her bottle of juice in hand. Before we knew it, we were off into the clouds. Isaac was grinning from ear to ear. He reached over, gently turned my head and kissed me. I put my hand on his knee. Shantel had the luxury of sitting in the window in her car seat, as though she knew what was going on. I sat there and was able to exhale.

"Thank You Lord," I gave due praise.

After landing in Florida, we grabbed our bags from the luggage claim. The kids were just as fascinated about that as they had been about the flight itself. You would have thought we never took the kids anywhere. We traveled many places over the years. We never had flown. With bags in hand, we rushed to catch the shuttle which took us straight to our Disney Resort.

"Mom, can we skip birthdays every year and make it up when school is out every summer?" JaRon felt bold enough to make the proposal.

"Ha ha, that's a good one," Isaac interrupted before I could respond.

"Yeah, that is smart thinking JaRon, but we much rather celebrate your birthdays when they get here. Who knows maybe we can consider future vacations as such, how about that?" I bargained.

"That will be awesome!" JaRon replied, pleased with the resolution to his proposal.

The first night in the resort was spectacular. Isaac booked a Wizard of Oz room, since the three oldest loved the movie so much. There was no getting away from the Wizard of Oz. Whomever came up with the ideas for the rooms must have been pure geniuses. As we entered the room, we were taken by the yellow brick road. The wall ahead was in the décor of the Cowardly Lion, Tin Man, Scarecrow, Dorothy, and Toto. If we hadn't known better, we would have walked up to the wall and bumped right into it. It appeared so real. The suite had two

229

beds up front, decorated with sparkly black comforters. The sparkles were purple and silver with greens and pinks.

The master suite was indeed Emerald City. The walls were green. There were ruby colored end tables on each side of the bed. The floor appeared like gold coins. It was a flat and smooth surface, but the illusion caused it to appear as though it was raised like you could just reach down and pick up a coin. The bathroom was too fancy for words. The mirror alone would have made one think they were in a palace. The chandelier affect would have made any little girl or woman of any age feel like a queen. Oh my, I had never seen a crystal-clear toilet in my life! It was almost too beautiful to sit on, let alone poop in.

The kids were on the verge of losing it. We called a little family huddle in attempt to calm them. It was insane! Too good to be true. Isaac reminded them the days ahead would be just as mind blowing. He informed them it was okay to take everything in, but to use their inside voices. Danielle was in shock. I am not sure she heard a word. She didn't realize she would be sleeping in the sparkly bed.

She asked, "Where are the beds for us to sleep in?"

Isaac and I chuckled so hard. Absolutely a stunning resort! The kids deserved the getaway. Shantel was awed as well. Her eyes were so big; she was looking around fascinated just like the kids. Isaac put her down and she started following the yellow brick road. A sight to see!

We took the kids to the swimming pool where the amazement continued. They played around for about an hour before we came back to our one room mansion. Isaac allowed Isaac Jr. to call room service. He ordered up a pizza. We ate the pizza on "the road" and discussed our plans for the days to come. Shantel was the first one to fall asleep, then Danielle, followed by JaRon and Isaac Jr. I guess they felt like they had to drift off in the order of their age. I must have fallen asleep before Isaac. I recalled taking a shower, getting in the bed, and before I knew it, I was waking up Thursday morning.

Vacation Continued

Thursday and Friday were spent at the theme park. There was no way to make a complete round through the park in one day. We didn't make a complete round through the park after the second day either. There was just so much to do. We would have needed at least two more days to make it around the entire theme park. Isaac had intended to get the kids VIP passes to get through the lines quicker, but he said he must have clicked on the wrong package. There was one with the option and one without, evidently, he picked the one without. We kept that little part a secret from the kids.

Isaac Jr. must have wanted to stop and take a picture every second. If I said he took less than one hundred pictures a day, I'd be lying. He was snap happy. One thing for sure, we agreed not to split up. When it was Shantel's turn to be in "Baby World," the kids had to enjoy Baby World right along with her. When Danielle wanted to stop in "Cinderella World," the other kids had to enjoy Cinderella World too.

When the boys wanted to visit "Harry Potter World" …you get the follow up routine.

The kids went from riding on rides and meeting Disney characters, to eating corn dogs, candied apples, cotton candy…junk food galore. There were no moments of boredom. Bathroom breaks were few, and they were mostly because Shantel needed to be changed. We knew better than to not make the kids attempt to go.

Quintella called Isaac a few times. He answered after the third call, instead of the first. Once he found out that she was "just checking," he told her he would have Shantel call once at night and he would call her himself if anything needed to be reported.

Basically, *my* man was saying, "Don't call just to be calling. You know we are on vacation. Shantel is fine. I'll let her say goodnight every night. I'll call you if I need to. Bye!"

That was my summary. I was impressed. Dr. Gregg deserved double pay.

Saturday morning, we awakened and got dressed. We hopped on the shuttle. We got off at a local shopping center that had a variety of Disney stores. We didn't allow the kids to buy souvenirs at the park because we didn't want to end up carrying any more than we had to. We allowed them to pick out a few souvenirs during shopping. Isaac gave them one hundred dollars each. We picked out Shantel a Minnie Mouse hat and sunglasses. She also got a big Minnie Mouse stuffed animal…too big for her little hands. I did ask Isaac would he be sending it home. I wanted to make sure his answer would be "no" as expected. It was. I knew then we'd be on the same page from that moment on. Isaac's backbone was locked in.

After shopping we took a trolley to the movie theater. The kids had never been in a thrill theater where the movie came to life right before their very eyes. I loved seeing their little faces in their 3D glasses, while their seats were just a bobbling away. Then…boom! Water shot out at the kids as one character on the screen threw a bucket of water at another character. The kids jumped. They oohed and awed, and they were tickled pink. Unfortunately, it was too much for Shantel. She began to holler. Isaac had to take her out. There were three back to back movies for one price. They each lasted five to eight minutes. Isaac and Shantel ended up missing out on the remainder.

After the movie, JaRon yelled, "This is the best vacation ever!"

I didn't see how anyone could possibly get upset about anything on a Disney vacation. A person would have to had literally been born mean and hateful to not have a good time. All my troubles had been washed away. We were in la la land, in a magical world. Truly, a once in a lifetime vacation for the Singleton family. If I had known what a blast it would have been, we would have taken a Disney trip much earlier. With exception of Shantel though, at least the kids were at an age where they would be able to recall the trip for the rest of their lives.

We met back up with Isaac and Shantel, waited on the next shuttle to take us back to the resort, hopped on, and hopped back off once we reached our destination. We spent the rest of our night in the room. The kids played with their souvenirs. Shantel walked around touching anything and everything. One thing about it, the room was safe and toddler proof. The outlets were covered. The furniture didn't have any sharp edges. She was free to roam. Like I said, whomever came up with the design was a pure genius.

Early Sunday morning, we shuttled back to the airport. We hated to leave but knew the day would come to return home. The kids decided to sit in the same order as prior. It was funny, the main one who said he wasn't going to go the sleep on the way, was the first one to go to sleep on the way back home. Isaac Jr. was tired! No pictures on the return. I had no clue why Danielle began to sing, "the wheels on the bus go round and round," but I let her have her way. She was happy, and I was cool with that. Isaac and Shantel drifted off at some point during the flight. I was exhausted but didn't want to sleep knowing Danielle and JaRon were up. Knowing me, I would have not fallen asleep even if they were asleep.

We are Family

A week had gone by and the kids were still talking about the family vacation. Everyone had a blast. It was not Shantel's weekend, but I kind of wished she were around. She was walking steadily and beginning to speak little words such as "no," and "stop." They may have not been the most positive, but she sure was cute when she said them. Knowing her little butt, she knew exactly what she was saying. She was inquisitive from the start, definitely a smart little girl.

Quintella tried to have a little attitude when Isaac didn't send any souvenirs home. Isaac was considerate enough to have a few pictures printed from Jr.'s camera. Personally, I thought that was reasonable. She could have been more appreciative. Obviously, she realized she could no longer manipulate things. Isaac had shut that down by following Dr. Gregg's recommendations. Like she said, he "conditioned" her. I didn't have any reasons to trip about anything because I was pleased with how Isaac had been handling everything. It proved a person can only do to you what you allow. Lord knows,

Willie Mae used to preach on that throughout her years. She sure knew a lot!

The kids were under the impression they were going to watch a movie. What they didn't know was when Isaac had taken Jr.'s camera and printed off a few pictures of Shantel, he also had a video created using all of the photos he had ever taken. There had to have been at least a thousand or so. There was some sort of program that allowed Isaac to coordinate music with sections of the photos based on what they were. I am glad he knew how to do all that fancy stuff because I had no clue.

Isaac and I spent the prior night watching the video. We wanted to make sure it would be as thrilling as possible. It turned out extremely nice! We couldn't wait to surprise the kids. Isaac Jr. had taken some excellent pictures. We could see him being a professional photographer one day. He would be just like his grandpa.

We all dressed in our family jammies. They consisted of different shades of purple. Well…white was included too; not everything was purple. Isaac purchased a coordinating purple hat. He loved him some hats. I stood out the most with my pinkish-red house socks. Believe it or not, one day while I was out shopping, I actually found a purple sofa chair. Purple was Willie Mae's favorite color. She liked green too, but I believe purple was her favorite of the two. Yes, I even found a purple bookshelf. I guess you can say I was a little overkill on the purple. It was what it was.

Danielle sat next to her dad. She used to sit next to me. I guess my shadow was either growing up, or she just felt the need to sit by her dad. I was cool with that. JaRon sat next to me. He oversaw the popcorn. The last time Danielle oversaw the popcorn she ended up spilling it. Isaac Jr. sat in his favorite spot on the floor. I never understood how he found the floor to be so comfortable. He would sit there with his legs folded and his back arched like he was meditating or something.

I decided I'd throw on my hair net and wig I got from Pebble's Weave and Wig Beauty Store. If I had known it was going to be so comfortable, I would have bought two identical ones. Isaac with the remote in hand, turned on the power to the DVD player. The kids thought they were about to watch "The Karate Kid." You can imagine who chose the movie. He won by a coin toss. At least it was not the "Wizard of Oz." Little did they know…

"What… *The Life of the Singletons*?" JaRon questioned, as he read the title as it appeared on the screen.

"Hey, this is not The Karate Kid," Danielle added.

"Y'all trying to trick us," Isaac Jr. said, the first to call Isaac and me out.

"How about a movie about the Singleton family," Isaac announced, more as an introduction rather than a question.

The kids were excited to see the Singleton movie. Isaac Jr. was surprised the most. All the pictures he took were right in front of his eyes.

"How did you do this?" JaRon asked, looking at Isaac Jr.

"I didn't do it," Jr. responded.

Danielle, already into the first picture, said, "Hey, that is me when I was a baby!"

My little shadow cracked me up the most. She kind of hung out in her own little world from time to time though.

We gobbled down the popcorn as we watched the family video. The kids were ecstatic, just as we imagined. The night could have not gone any better; but every now and then, I had some weird thoughts cross my mind. The thoughts always came whenever we had movie time or family time in the living room.

The devil is a liar!

I did my best to tune out the thoughts and to enjoy my family. Isaac sat proud like a king. He was. I imagine if he was the king, I was the queen. Isaac Jr. and JaRon were each a prince. And Danielle, from day one, was indeed the princess.

After the family video, we ended up watching "The Karate Kid" after all. JaRon felt the need to hop off the sofa at every chopping moment. He was so funny. All the kids had a unique sense of humor. I guess that's where I got mine. Isaac was not much of a jokester, every now and then he tried. I think the kids would just laugh to make him feel special.

The weekend was lovely. I really enjoyed spending time with Isaac and the kids. It reminded me of how things were many years ago. Things seemed to have finally gotten back to where they used to be. Even though I still couldn't quite grasp why something was trying to steal my joy, I managed to take everything to heart. I was profoundly grateful. I had my little family back. The kids deserved it and so did I. The song, "We are Family," popped up in my head. Boy did I love that song back in the day. In our case, the lyrics would have been, "We are family. I got my kids and my husband with me."

Reflections

My life in a nutshell. When I saw Isaac in high school, I only knew he was charming, he was a star football player, and he could run fast. Did I know what type of grades he made? No. Did I know any future ambitions? No. I didn't know much about Isaac. As a matter of fact, I didn't know much about myself. Who was I? I was someone who plotted to get *my* dream man. Welp, I got him. That was it. A stranger to myself, I hated school and had no plans beyond high school. As far as friends, I'd say I had about one or two.

Sure, I married Isaac based off the fact he was handsome. Luckily, from what I could gather, everything worked out fine for nine years. I learned a little more about him along the way. One thing for sure, he was a hard worker. He provided. He was blessed with an inheritance, which boosted our ability to invest in a nice home and have two nice cars and an old truck. I didn't want for anything much other than *my* sexy chocolate.

I learned that I had little to no respect for myself. Everything and anything bothered me. Hell, I'll admit it, I was flat out crazy! It had to been all me. I was raised with high morals and values. Where did I get lost? Beats me.

Isaac's affair was an eye opener. It taught me anything could happen to anyone, at any time. Good people…crazy people…anybody.

Isaac was my all and all. I thought for sure I was his all and all, but he still had an affair. I saw how easy circumstances could lead to cheating. I almost had an affair myself.

I spent most of my life judging people. Unfortunately, I'd have to say I spent a lot of my time "mis"-judging people. I misjudged Sophia. I misjudged Gina. At one point, I misjudged Benjamin. Come to find out, out of all people, I misjudged the very person living under the same roof, my husband of nine plus years. He could do no wrong. He was perfect. No flaws.

Despite the madness, I considered myself a decent mother. I prayed the kids wouldn't pick up any negativity from me. I prayed their future lives would not be the same. Willie Mae did a marvelous job. She taught me everything I needed to know growing up. I may have failed to apply the learning in a timely manner, causing me to suffer when the time came to utilize what was instilled. I was brought up in church. Lord knows I knew God was everything. Being God, He allowed me to hit my rock bottom, therefore, all I could do was look up. In the end I was reminded to worship Him and not Isaac. Sad it took years, but better late than never, huh?

In conclusion, believe it or not, Isaac and I ended up going our separate ways. We divorced about three months after our family vacation of a lifetime. You see, after our last family night, it finally dawned on me, the lady in the picture on our living room wall was yet another lady who Isaac had gotten pregnant. Put it this way—the picture was there but not there. It was all in my imagination. Every time we gathered as a family; I had a vivid picture in the back of my mind. The same lady. The same scene.

All along, though behind me, I had the biggest clue right in front of my very eyes. So, the bottom line is, yes, Isaac cheated again. This time he had an affair with one of the youth teachers at the new church, Danielle's youth teacher! I never saw it coming. I have said repeatedly that Isaac was a slickster. He was who Michael Jackson would have referred to as a "smooth criminal." Player indeed.

Ms. Robinson came marching into church one Sunday morning wearing her pinkish-red dress and updo hairstyle. She boldly marched right up to Isaac in my presence.

"Do you want to tell her, or do you want me to?" she threatened.

That was the end of that story. I didn't ask any questions. I didn't feel the need. I didn't curse. I didn't act a fool. Instead, I calmly headed straight to children's church, picked up the kids, and left. On the way home, I explained to the kids that Isaac and I needed to separate again. I assured them we would sit down and talk in detail. I went home and I started packing.

A few days later, I was able to find a rental house 115 miles away, about five miles from my father. I took the first job I could get, which was as a waitress for a nearby restaurant. I held my head up and did what I needed to do. Once settled, I sent Isaac my information so he could send monies my way. I informed him that *he* could drive to pick up the kids whenever he wanted. I wished him well on his having babies by church ladies adventures.

I found out later a lot of Isaac's customers were lovers as well. Face it, not only did I marry a high school quarterback and All-American track star, but also, I married an All-American game player. One who played me for many years. But guess what? I was okay with it. Like Ms. Joyce Ann told me before I left, "His loss!"

It was not like she hadn't warned me. She had previously mentioned "it was not over." She apologized. She just didn't realize her prediction of "more to come" would boil down to it being another affair.

God came on time like I had been told He would. I was saddened by the situation; however, I had a sense of contentment at the same time. I had finally given my 100%. I was cool with that. I had nothing else to offer. I would say I'd have to disagree with the statement, "If it happens once shame on them. If it happens again shame on you." I'd say shame on Isaac twice!

After all, I had the final victory. I ended up with someone who appreciated me and someone who knew what it was like to be screwed. Benjamin brought out the best in me. *My* Benji!

"Thank You Lord for Benjamin Michael. You work in mysterious ways," I praised God.

After about six months of talking to Benjamin long distance, and explaining future plans with the kids, he ended up moving in with me. After his lease was up, he moved in with Sophia after their talk following Shantel's party, but they had mutually agreed there was nothing between them. Sophia had two extra rooms. She wanted to relieve him from his misery of being used and abused by Michelle Lee, so she allowed Benjamin to rent one of the rooms.

In the meantime, Michelle Lee pretty much cut Benjamin from parental privileges. He had to fight in court to be rewarded visitation. Due to distance, he was only awarded one weekend a month, and holidays every other year. He was granted the opportunity to keep Destiny two weeks every summer. The judge granted Destiny Benjamin's last name. So, Destiny *Who* became Destiny Michael. Quintella's and Michelle's scheme didn't play all the way out as they expected.

Eleven months after Benjamin relocated, Evette Singleton became Evette Michael. The kids and I lived happily ever after. For the third time, we found a church. Benjamin landed a job as a manager at a local food mart due to his previous experience. We survived. We made enough income to pay our bills. We made enough income to eat out from time to time. We made enough income to go on family outings at least twice a year. Above all, we had genuine love for one another, and the kids adjusted well. No doubt, I had the best kids ever! And sista girl ended up with the best guy in the whole wide world: Mr. Benjamin Michael, a hard worker, a loving father, and a loving stepfather. Most of all, Benjamin was a faithful husband. *My soulmate.* Till death do us part!

I dedicate this page to my father, Marvin L. Sample, Sr.; my husband, Isiah Mack; my son, Kendall Sample; and my daughter, TaShauna Etherington. It is because of each of you that I was able to accomplish what I have accomplished thus far in life.

This picture means the world to me!

Grandfather and grandson saluting one another.

My dad, an Army Veteran, served in the Vietnam War in 1966. Thank you for your service.

My son, an Oklahoma Air National Guardsman, has served since 2019. Thank you for your willingness to serve.

My brother, Marvin Sample, Jr., an Army Veteran (not pictured), served in Operation Iraqi Freedom War in 2007. Thank you for your service.

Made in the USA
Coppell, TX
20 November 2021

66074652R00150